W9-BIP-245

A GIANT WIN

A GIANT WIN

INSIDE THE NEW YORK GIANTS'
HISTORIC UPSET OVER
THE NEW ENGLAND PATRIOTS IN
SUPER BOWL XLII

TOM COUGHLIN

with Greg Hanlon

Foreword by Eli Manning

GRAND CENTRAL
PUBLISHING

NEW YORK   BOSTON

Grand Central Publishing
Hachette Book Group
1290 Avenue of the Americas, New York, NY 10104
grandcentralpublishing.com
twitter.com/grandcentralpub

First Edition: December 2022

Grand Central Publishing is a division of Hachette Book Group, Inc. The Grand Central Publishing name and logo is a trademark of Hachette Book Group, Inc.

The publisher is not responsible for websites (or their content) that are not owned by the publisher.

The Hachette Speakers Bureau provides a wide range of authors for speaking events. To find out more, go to www.hachettespeakersbureau.com or call (866) 376-6591.

Library of Congress Cataloging-in-Publication Data
Names: Coughlin, Tom (Thomas Richard), 1946- author. | Hanlon, Greg
    (Editor) author. | Manning, Eli, 1981- author.
Title: A Giant win : inside the New York Giants' historic upset over the New
    England Patriots in Super Bowl XLII / Tom Coughlin with Greg Hanlon ;
    foreword by Eli Manning.
Description: First edition. | New York, N.Y. : Grand Central Publishing, 2022.
Identifiers: LCCN 2022031711 | ISBN 9781538724644 (hardcover) |
    ISBN 9781538724668 (ebook)
Subjects: LCSH: Super Bowl (42nd : 2008 : University of Phoenix Stadium,
    Glendale, Ariz.) | New York Giants (Football team)—History. | New
    England Patriots (Football team)—History. | Coughlin, Tom (Thomas
    Richard), 1946- | Football coaches—United States—Biography.
Classification: LCC GV956.2.S8 C68 2022 | DDC
    796.332/64097471—dc23/eng/20220810
LC record available at https://lccn.loc.gov/2022031711

ISBNs: 9781538724644 (hardcover), 9781538724668 (ebook)

Printed in Canada

MRQ-T

10 9 8 7 6 5 4 3 2 1

Tom Coughlin

For Judy. The real champion.
One ring means more to me than the others.

Greg Hanlon

For my family.

CONTENTS

Foreword by Eli Manning   ix

Introduction: The Practice Battles of 1990   1

One: Our First Drive, and Our Quarterback   13

Two: Last Year It Was My Ass   43

Three: The War Hero Who Helped Get Us Here   79

Four: A Good O-Line Is Like a Symphony   99

Five: You Have to Knock Tom Brady Down   119

Six: Where I Come From, Who I Am   155

Seven: Kevin Boss and the Rookie Brigade
to the Rescue   179

Eight: Hail to the Achievers   191

Nine: The Drive That Binds Us Together,
Forever   211

Ten: Canyon of Heroes   237

Epilogue: Judy   247

Acknowledgments   265

About the Authors   273

FOREWORD

by Eli Manning

I was a backup for my first NFL game, in September 2004 against Philadelphia, but Coach Coughlin gave me an assignment: I had to watch every single blitz the Eagles ran in preseason and diagram them all in a notebook. Then I had to draw up what my call would be for each of those blitzes against our five main pass protections.

Then I had to do the same thing the next week, and the next week, and the next week. Pretty soon I was diagramming three hundred plays per week. One time, I let up a bit and thought to myself, *There's no way he's actually looking at every page of this*, and just scribbled something down without thinking too much.

My notebook came back full of red ink.

Play tracking was tedious and exhausting—but

it was absolutely necessary, and it was the most important lesson Coach Coughlin taught me: Who wins or loses a football game is determined by who pushes past the tedium and exhaustion to get the little things right. That's why Coach Coughlin and I won two Super Bowls together. That's why he should be in the Hall of Fame.

I spent twelve years with Coach Coughlin after coming to New York with him in 2004, and I always felt we were in the same boat. We won together, we lost together, the papers sometimes wanted to run us out of town together—and we stood at the podium and raised those Lombardi Trophies together. During those twelve years, his mentality never changed: The circumstances didn't matter; what people were saying about us on the outside didn't matter. The only thing that mattered was the upcoming opponent and the work that had to be done to beat them.

By 2007, our whole team had bought into his mindset, taking on the identity of a group that persevered through adversity by putting our heads down and going to work. That season had some rough patches: We started off 0-2, and the chatter started up (again) that Coach Coughlin should be fired. I struggled for a few games late in the regular season, and people were saying I was a bust. We blocked it out, made corrections, and worked through all of it.

Personality-wise, Coach Coughlin and I are very different, but we're wired the same way—we were all about preparation, paying attention to the small things, and putting team above self. I'd like to think I came to New York with these qualities, but it's honestly hard for me to say how much I was already like this and how much Coach Coughlin rubbed off on me. He was *that* formative of an influence. When I met him, I was a twenty-three-year-old kid coming to New York and wanting desperately to succeed. By the end of our time together, I was a thirty-five-year-old father and husband.

Most of our time was spent immersed in football, in all those details that went into our preparation. But as the years went by, I saw another side of the man. The guy who'd ask you about your family, or talk glowingly about his grandkids, or crack a joke and show you that yes, Tom Coughlin is actually very funny. I always respected his dedication to his job, but as the years went on, I saw his commitment to his family, his charity supporting families of children with cancer, and his faith. Those are his fundamental values, and they're mine as well.

Our time in New York together wasn't always easy. But I came to learn that New Yorkers respect you *more* when that's the case. They can identify with the guy who goes through tough times but manages to work his way through it. The guy who gets knocked down but keeps getting back up. Coach Coughlin and I did that, and we brought the city and the region two championships. Now *that's* a great New York story.

And it was all the product of the thousands of little details we worked so hard to get down cold. Like the blitz recognition and protections I diagrammed in a book before my first career game in 2004, in Philadelphia.

Fast-forward now to February 3, 2008, in Glendale, Arizona. We're down 14–10; there's thirty-nine seconds left on the clock and we're at the Patriots' 13-yard line, needing a touchdown to win. The Patriots call an all-out blitz—rushing seven against our five offensive linemen and running back Brandon Jacobs. But we're prepared for it, and I know Brandon will scan the defensive front and pick up the free rusher coming off the right side and into my face. On Tom Coughlin–coached teams, these things don't get missed.

Because I know our blocking will hold up for *just* enough time, I don't have to rush my throw to Plaxico Burress, who's running a fade on the left side. And because my throw is not rushed, Plaxico has time to fake a slant inside before getting into his fade. And because Plaxico makes this inside slant move, Patriots cornerback Ellis Hobbs has to bite on it, leaving Plaxico wide open on the fade.

Plaxico catches the ball in the end zone, we become champions, and Super Bowl XLII becomes the first game people think of when they think of me and Coach Coughlin. We were in the same boat when we came to the Giants in 2004, and now we're in the same boat in history. And I couldn't be prouder of that.

Introduction

THE PRACTICE BATTLES
OF 1990

The first thing I noticed about Bill Belichick was that his work ethic was a lot like mine. He was an early-morning guy and I was, too. After practices, when the coaching staff met and Bill Parcells peppered us with questions about player assignments, he was on top of every detail. I'm a detail guy, too.

It was the late 1980s. I'd been hired by Parcells to be the wide receivers coach of the New York Giants. Parcells had a big personality and his trademark sense of humor, but he ran a tight ship, and nothing ever got in the way of the work. Practices and meetings were brisk and direct. Bang, bang. No nonsense, no laxity, no patience for excuses.

In other words, it was the best place possible for an aspiring head coach to apprentice, and that was what Belichick and I were doing. There were lots of talented coaches in that room—Belichick, the defensive coordinator and secondary coach; Romeo Crennel, the special teams and defensive line coach; Charlie Weis, a special teams assistant; to name a few—and all of us were like sponges.

We also shared one belief: Competition brought out the best in people. With this in mind, Bill and I sought each other out to get our players extra work. My receivers and his defensive backs would go at each other, over and over, making each other better every day. If I needed my guys to see a live press coverage, I'd tell Bill and he'd give it to me. If he needed a pattern so his guys could work on a certain coverage, I'd give it to him.

One evening in training camp, as we were planning the next day's practice, we asked Parcells if the receivers and d-backs could do more one-on-one work in the tight red zone. He shot us a look: *You two? You guys wanna do that again!?* We always did. There was no end to our appetite for trying to get better.

That was what types of coaches we were. It was a principle that Parcells stressed: For us to win, every man along the chain of command had to do his job to the best of his ability. As assistant coaches, it made us feel valued, and it underscored that we were part of something bigger than ourselves. Every person was important, and so was every*thing*—including those training camp reps Bill and I ran against each other again and again.

The hard work paid off. We won the Super Bowl in 1990. Parcells became a legend in New York. And to astute fans, so did Belichick, whose defense limited Joe Montana's 49ers to thirteen points in the NFC Championship game, and then held the juggernaut Bills to nineteen points in the Super Bowl. Belichick's defensive game plan for the Super Bowl is displayed in the Pro Football Hall of Fame.

I took pride in knowing my receivers contributed to those outstanding defensive performances. But they did much more than that: In the final moments of the 49ers game, Stephen Baker made a double move along the sideline and caught a thirteen-yard pass that set up our game-winning field goal. In the Super Bowl, on a critical third-down play on a third-quarter touchdown drive that gave us the lead, Mark Ingram got the first down by juking five defenders who had a good shot at him. It was a play that symbolized the extra effort expected of every man on those Giants teams.

After the game, I told Mark he'd just made the greatest nonscoring play in the history of the Super Bowl. At the time, that was true.

From the moment I got hired by Bill Parcells in '88, I felt a sense of almost spiritual kinship with the Giants organization. A sense that I was *home*.

It all started at the top with the owner, Wellington Mara, and later, Bob Tisch as well. Both were old-fashioned guys with strong moral principles, the type of person I strive to be. I can fill a book with stories about those two men, but one story about Mr. Mara, delivered by John Mara in his eulogy at his dad's funeral, says it all: Every year at Christmastime when John was growing up, Mr. Mara would hang the parish's confession schedule on the fridge with a little note: *No confession, no Santa.* First things first. Work before play. Those were his values and those were the Giants' values and those were my values.

I liked Bill Parcells from the beginning as well. We first met in Mobile, Alabama, where Parcells was scouting at the Senior Bowl, and I went down to interview with him. (I'd spent the previous two years in Green Bay, but then our head coach, Forrest Gregg, left to coach in college.) I had another interview in Mobile, with the Steelers' Hall of Fame coach, Chuck Noll, and Coach Noll and I met over dinner. But Parcells was a lot more informal: We met in the lobby of his hotel and then went upstairs to his room to talk for about an hour.

He didn't waste any time, because he never did. He wanted a coach who had energy, and he wanted to hear details of what I could bring to the table. He was considering me for both the tight ends coach and the wide receivers coach job, but I wanted the receivers job, and we talked in depth about techniques I would teach—the little things that don't make it into the media narratives but the things that actually win or lose football games. I told him I'd developed a technique to beat bump-and-run coverage that involved determining leverage and executing the proper footwork. I told him about how to practice catching the ball with your hands away from your body, and zeroing in on the tip of the ball, likening it to the way Larry Bird focused on one eyelet on the rim when he shot the basketball. I told him I believed wide receivers were also blockers, which obviously fit into the Giants' run-heavy offense at the time.

He offered me the job and so did Coach Noll; I chose the Giants over the Steelers. The Giants had won the Super Bowl the season before last, and the core was in place to win more. I was in my early forties and I'd been in the league for four years, and I was proud of the work I'd done in my stops in Green

Bay and, before that, Philadelphia. But I hadn't won. It was about time I started.

There's a mystique about New York and an aura around the Giants as a proud franchise, which I bought into wholeheartedly. When I came to the Giants, I felt like I'd finally arrived. I'd grown up in Waterloo, New York, population 4,400 back then, 260 miles northwest of the city, and New York had always been a lodestar. My grandfather was a Yankees fanatic who'd seen Gehrig and Ruth play. As a young man I'd admired the great Knicks teams with Frazier, Bradley, and DeBusschere for their selflessness and the way they captivated the city. The Giants, by 1988, were in the middle of a run just like that. It was a proud feeling to walk out of the tunnel of Giants Stadium and see the immensity of the building, with the New York crowd and their singular passion.

Working on Parcells's staff was a great learning experience. He knew exactly the type of football he wanted to play—strong defense, a physical running game with some play-action passes—and he didn't overcomplicate things. He made it clear we weren't reinventing the wheel. His whole mantra was: *Give them a good plan and let them play*. The results spoke for themselves.

He was a very unique person, one of those guys who made it his business to know an awful lot about a lot of things, especially with sports. He'd go to boxing matches at Madison Square Garden with Romeo Crennel and he could tell you the entire Chicago Cubs infield from decades before. He knew the complete fifty-three-man roster of every NFL team we played, partly because he was super prepared, but also because he really just loved sports. He would talk with me about my college coach at Syracuse, the great Ben Schwartzwalder, and kid me about the gray socks Syracuse teams always wore. And even though there was never any wasted time in his meetings and practices, he always found time to relate to us as people. Sometimes, when the other offensive assistants and I were doing preparation work in an offensive staff room, he'd come in and shoot the breeze for a few minutes. It was understood we'd put our pens down and listen to him. Whatever story he'd tell, it was always interesting.

Still, I was an assistant, and all assistant coaches want to be head coaches. I'd set a goal for myself to become a head coach by the age of forty-five, and during the '90 season, when I was forty-four, Boston College contacted me in the middle of the season and assessed my interest in their head coaching job. At the time, the Giants were 10-0, and I didn't want to become a distraction to our team, but I talked with Parcells and he was terrific about it, telling me I could go through the interview process and trusting me to keep my focus on the Giants. I'd been an assistant with BC in the early '80s and I loved the place for similar reasons I loved the Giants: I liked its strong Jesuit academics, its tradition, and its emphasis on values. Its *solidness*.

After we won that Super Bowl, I hit the recruiting trail as BC's new head coach, and I wasn't the only Giants coach to leave. Belichick became the head coach of the Cleveland Browns, and Parcells retired.

Fourteen years went by. I had many great experiences, which I'll discuss at length later. But by 2003 I was out of a job again. I've always believed that luck is when preparation meets opportunity, so I spent that season preparing for my next chance to be a head coach in the NFL, which I had faith would come. I barricaded myself in a room every Sunday to watch games and then had the coaches' tapes delivered to my house every week. I paid my own way to the scouting combine in Indianapolis, stopwatch around my neck. I wasn't a head coach in the league, but I prepared like one.

Late in the 2003 season, John Mara called me. The Giants were struggling, and everyone knew they'd be moving on from Jim Fassel, including Fassel himself, who asked the organization to announce his firing but allow him to coach the season's last two games. Fassel had taken the Giants to the Super Bowl three years before, but by '03 the roster was depleted and riddled with injuries, and the team finished 4-12. Despite that, I knew in my bones this was the opportunity I had prepared for. This was the New York Giants.

I went through the interview process and was as impressed with the organization as I'd been thirteen years before. The Giants interviewed other candidates—two of whom, Romeo Crennel and Charlie Weis, were also on the 1990 staff—but they offered me the job and I accepted.

Wellington Mara greeted me when I got to New Jersey.

—*Welcome home,* he said.

———

Fast-forward four years. A lot happened in the interim. Wellington Mara and Bob Tisch passed away within weeks of each other in 2005. That year, we restored a sense of pride in the organization and won the division. But we slipped to 8-8 the following season, which ended bitterly. The media wanted to run me out of town on a rail, and the players' relationship with the press wasn't much better. When we started off the '07 season at 0-2, there wasn't a pundit who didn't leave our team, and my career, for dead.

But we didn't give up on ourselves, and on

January 28, 2008, an airplane carrying the improbable NFC Champion New York Giants touched down in Phoenix Sky Harbor International Airport. The TV cameras captured the players stepping out onto the tarmac wearing all-black suits, many with sunglasses. The media learned the players wore the suits as an in-joke: They were dressed for the Patriots' "funeral"—as in, the funeral for their undefeated season.

I didn't like the gesture but by then I'd decided to yield a bit more to my veteran players, so I let it slide, provided we didn't give it oxygen by talking about it with the media. The players rewarded my faith with an outstanding week of practice. We had the focus and confidence of a team that had been through a lot but had come out the other side.

But we were under no illusions about the difficulty of our task: In six days, on the other side of the field, would be the New England Patriots. They were 18-0, already the best record in the NFL's history. Their 589 points during the regular season made them the greatest scoring machine of all time. Their coach was Bill Belichick.

Limiting distractions was my goal, and to that end we caught a break with the team hotel the NFL assigned to us: the Sheraton Wild Horse Pass Resort & Spa in Chandler, in the middle of the desert, twenty miles from downtown Phoenix. All the restaurants were on-site. The first two nights there, I gave my players a late curfew. Some guys went out that first night but it was such a hassle that nobody went out the second. When Fox broadcaster Troy Aikman came to our hotel for our pregame briefing, he kidded: *This looks like a Tom Coughlin hotel choice.*

Meanwhile, the league had put the Patriots in downtown Phoenix. Near the action, near the media. We took that as another hint that to the NFL, the Patriots were the main attraction. That the game itself was a foregone conclusion, a formality before the Patriots' coronation as the best team ever.

By that point, we had grown accustomed to tuning out media narratives. There was a calm and peace about our approach that week, a confidence that we deserved to be there, despite what everyone else thought. I encouraged our guys to enjoy themselves, to be in the moment, to do their work, and to avoid distractions.

This was true for me as well. Early on the morning of the game, I was at my desk in my hotel suite when a pack of my grandkids knocked on the door. A bunch of them started climbing all over me, and my granddaughter got into my game-plan notes and started coloring all over them.

I just laughed—and I stepped outside myself and noted that I *laughed*, that I was *enjoying* myself. I was at peace, grateful to be coaching that day just like I was grateful for my grandkids. Not too long ago, I'd been a forty-four-year-old assistant in a windowless room in the old Giants Stadium, with Bill Belichick a few chairs down from me. We'd all come a long way on our journeys since then.

Chapter One

OUR FIRST DRIVE, AND OUR QUARTERBACK

If you want to know about me, if you want to know about Eli Manning, and if you want to know about the 2007 Giants, know this: Before each of our postseason games—Tampa Bay, Dallas, Green Bay, New England—none of the Fox studio panelists picked us to win any of them. Not a single panelist, not a single game. The expression "No one gave us a chance" is a cliché. In the case of the Fox guys and us, it was literally true.

It was yet another thing that pulled our team together. In previous years, the Giants' locker room had been thin-skinned and easily distractible, with some notable players airing their grievances in the media. But that poisonous atmosphere was a distant memory by the 2007 playoffs, and the negativity from the outside gave us a challenge we relished. That has always been my mentality—*Tell me I can't do something and I'll prove you wrong*—and by the playoffs, our whole team had taken on that attitude. In the two weeks of practice leading up to the Super Bowl, nearly everything the players did showed us as coaches that they were in the right frame of mind.

The same was true for Eli Manning. His confidence in himself and his teammates, and our confidence in him, was rock-solid. People had been doubting him his whole career. Now it was his turn to show who he really was.

By that point in his career, Eli was firmly in command of the offense. Under his belt were his four seasons in the league, our three-game playoff run, and even our Week 17 game against New England, when he played very well in a game we lost, 38–35. All of the tape study, and all of the subtle tweaks we had made along the way—he'd digested all of it. Now it was just a matter of doing what we knew he was capable of doing.

One moment from our week of practice in Arizona stood out. By now, it's lore among Giants fans that on the Friday before the Super Bowl, David Tyree had one of the worst practices in the history of the sport. Everything we threw to him, he dropped. Drop after drop after drop after drop. Everyone chuckled and laughed it off, not wanting to make too big a thing of it. But you never want to see a player be at their worst in the last live practice before the biggest game of their life.

Enter Eli. After practice was over, Eli went up to David. He told him to shake it off. He told him he knew he'd be there when we needed him most. Like everything Eli did, it was understated and didn't draw attention. But the coaching staff saw it, and we liked it. Eli knew David would be there for him, just like we knew Eli would be there for us.

———

Game time approaches. The days, then the hours, then the minutes.

During pregame stretching, I go around to every player and acknowledge them, either by shaking their hand or tapping them on the shoulder. It's a routine I'd been doing for years, a final reminder that we're all in this together. The guys are close to the competitive moment. You can tell how important this game is to them by the look in their eyes.

During warmups, my gaze drifts up to the stands, and I see a Giants fan in a T-shirt that says

"18-1." I get a kick out of that. I like that our fans are as confident as we are.

One thing on my mind before the game is the different timelines in the Super Bowl compared to other games for pregame festivities, commercials, and halftime—which is twenty-eight minutes, compared to twelve minutes during the regular season. This presents a challenge: Athletes are finely tuned machines, and we don't want the long pregame routine and halftime to take them out of their normal rhythm. Days before the game, I'd talked to Tony Dungy, a friend of mine, who stressed the importance of preserving your players' energy during these long lulls. There's a lot of nervous energy and it needs to be controlled, and it's the coaching staff's job to make sure the players are managing it. Our coaches instruct their positional groups to stay off their feet, to calm down, to not let their emotions overrun them. It's going to be a long night, and they're gonna need every last bit of energy they have.

After our time in the locker room, it's our turn to run out of the tunnel for the introductions on the public address system. As is our custom, we forgo individual player introductions and run out as a team, and I jog out beside the guys and take in the panorama of the University of Phoenix Stadium. The roof is closed, and up high in the building, there's something sparkling in the air. I would never know what it was exactly—Flashbulbs? A lighting effect in the stadium? My mind playing tricks on me?—but it underscores the magnitude and splendor of the moment. We are in the Super Bowl.

Then we wait. In a normal game, about seven and a half minutes elapses between the time we run onto the field and kickoff, and guys have their routines, like sprinting down to the end zone to fire up the crowd. But in the Super Bowl, there's twenty-two minutes of this in-between time, so we tell our players to sit on the bench and get back into energy conservation mode. We don't tell them to relax, exactly, because that would be impossible. But we want them, to the best of their ability, to settle themselves, to take in the scene, and to use this as a chance to appreciate where they are. This is the stuff they'll be telling their grandkids about decades from now.

I had said in my Saturday night speech before the game that when you win the Super Bowl, it's not just *you* who becomes a champion—it's also everyone who helped get you there. Your family, your friends, your coaches—they all come with you to the top of the mountain, where they stand a little taller. During our week in Arizona, our hotel pool was just outside my door, and I remember looking out and watching the players play with their kids. The Friday night before, we had a team family picnic on a Native American reservation, and all the families took hayrides to get there. Seeing our players in those settings, as opposed to the facility where we'd spent years grinding every day together, allowed our team to interact in a different way, and it enriched our relationships with each other. We're all so caught up with trying to win every week that it's easy to overlook that a football team is a family. At our Saturday night meeting, we played a video montage that conveyed the message we wanted to send, put together by our staff members Ed Triggs, Chris Pridy, and Kim Kolbe. It concluded with the Green Day song with that emotional refrain: "I hope you had the time of your life." As the minutes tick down to kickoff, I want the guys to realize: *This* is the time of our lives, so let's make the most of the opportunity.

I think about our game plan, which has four pillars: First, we have to pressure the quarterback and knock him off his spot. If Tom Brady feels comfortable, your defense is in for a long night.

Second, we can't let Randy Moss beat us with big plays. Getting pressure on Brady will help against Moss, because if Brady's pressured, he'll have to get the ball out of his hand before the deep route develops. But we'll also consistently roll coverages to

Moss's side, bracketing him inside and outside with double coverage.

Third, we have to run the ball with the goal of controlling the clock. Our previous game against New England had been close, but it was hardly the style of game we wanted to play—you don't want to get into a shootout with the 2007 Patriots. By limiting their possessions, we could make this a defensive-minded game, where we liked our chances.

Fourth, we have to avoid turnovers. During the 2007 postseason, our offense hadn't turned the ball over once, while our defense had generated six turnovers by the opposition. Against a team as high-powered as the Patriots, we couldn't afford to give them extra chances to score.

On the field, I looked at our guys. I know they're prepared, but now we need them to play above the X's and O's. I always like to say that in any football game, there are five plays that determine the outcome, and we have to make at least three of those plays. As I walk up and down the sideline looking at my players, I'm wondering who will step up and make one of those plays. Often, it's a guy you don't expect.

Finally at 4:32 p.m. MST, the wait is over: Amid thousands of flashbulbs, Patriots kicker Stephen Gostkowski boots the ball into the end zone. Our return man, Domenik Hixon, brings the ball out to our 23-yard line.

Eli Manning leads us onto the field. As has been the case every week during the playoffs, this is the biggest game of his career. As always, Eli is ready to go.

———

Nearly four years before, in early 2004, I was in New Orleans, at the Saints' indoor practice facility. Ole Miss quarterback Eli Manning would be working out for NFL teams before the draft with a group of receivers, and it seemed like every scout and talent evaluator had shown up to see the latest version of the great Manning family quarterbacks. But minutes before the appointed time, Eli wasn't there.

People looked at their watches, wondering where he was. Everyone was thinking the same thing: *If this were Peyton, he'd have been here hours ago.* The minutes ticked by before word trickled out about where he was: He'd stopped on the way to pick up a sandwich. He'd get there on time.

That was lesson number one about Eli: He does what he has to do in his uniquely composed, matter-of-fact way, always staying true to himself. He doesn't rush. He's got it under control.

After he got there, he said hi to a few people. His

demeanor, as ever, was kinda shy. Then he warmed up for a few minutes to get his arm ready. And then he proceeded to have one of the best workouts I can remember, blowing away everyone in that building with his arm talent: post corners, deep overs, gos, comebacks, outs, option routes to running backs, roll rights, roll lefts. Bing, bang, boom, everything on the money. It was a forty-minute workout, and maybe two balls hit the ground the entire time.

Then Eli walked off the field as unassumingly as he'd walked onto it. He nodded his head to a couple of people on the sideline and left.

That was lesson number two about Eli: If you're looking to make a snap assessment of him, you're gonna get him wrong.

———

Ernie Accorsi deserves the credit for making Eli a Giant. Leading up to the draft, he had five years of study on Eli and he stuck his neck out further than anyone else in our organization. His logic was simple, and the years since have proven him right: You can't win in this league without *a franchise quarterback*, as he'd always put it. He knew Eli was one, so he did what he had to do to get him to New York.

New York is tough, and so were the expectations that came with Eli's name. Fortunately, Eli's tough, too, and he learned how to deal with all of it. But that's not to say it was easy.

I remember the first day of his rookie minicamp: We threw a lot of the playbook at Eli, with new terminology. It was the first time he'd practiced as an NFL player and the first time he'd called out our quarterback cadence, and he had a ho-hum couple of days of practice. Not bad but not great. The writers noticed it, and after that one minicamp, they felt entitled to render a judgment in the papers the next day: The guy we'd given up a king's ransom for—namely, Philip Rivers, who we drafted knowing the San Diego Chargers wanted him, along with a third-round pick and a future first- and fifth-round pick—wasn't all that impressive.

Eli was a rookie quarterback and I was in my first year as the head coach of the Giants, and at that point, both of us were getting used to what we were in for. The New York media runs on snap judgments and negativity. It's a difficult place to play and coach, and it requires people who have an unshakable belief in themselves and are motivated to be the best they can be, regardless of what people are saying about them. I've always felt Eli and I share that core similarity, and that was what enabled us to have success together.

It was hard for the media to understand Eli, and

I think that was frustrating for them. But among our team, we knew what he was all about. All that rah-rah stuff, and the potshots about his body language? That's for the people on the outside who don't really know what's going on or understand the game's complexities. You see a lot of that in football: A lot of people watch and talk about the sport, but it's almost impossible for the average person to actually know what's happening on a given play, so it gets reduced to easy-to-understand narratives that have nothing to do with why teams win or lose. But *leadership* isn't yelling at your teammates on the field or giving some fiery speech. Leadership is *work*. It's the *example* you set.

And nobody set a better example than Eli. Yes, he was quiet and unassuming, but his work habits were second to none. Being a quarterback is an intellectually rigorous job, one that requires you to know the responsibilities of everyone on the field and to quickly size up what a defense is trying to do. Eli had everything down cold. Every Monday morning at 7 a.m., he'd be at the facility, reviewing the previous game. On Tuesday, when the rest of the players were off, Eli was studying the next opponent. Grinding. For the rest of the team, we gave the game plan out on Wednesday, but Eli always requested it on Tuesday and knew everyone else's assignments before they got in the next day. Not only was he a tremendous worker, he was also exceptionally smart—his 39 Wonderlic score was nearly double the NFL's average—and that was invaluable to us coaches. We knew we could throw anything at him and he'd master it quickly. There was no limit to what he could handle.

Another thing Eli did that allowed the coaching staff to best do our jobs: He played, every Sunday, for 210 straight games. People tend to give him a nice pat on the back for this, but I doubt they truly appreciate what an accomplishment this is given the violence of the sport and the caliber of athletes out there. Some of it is luck, sure: Eli was fortunate to never take that big hit to his knee that could have ended a season. But as Branch Rickey always used to say, "Luck is the residue of design." In Eli's case, he avoided the most dangerous situations because he was incredibly prepared. And he was incredibly tough: Case in point, the beginning of the 2007 season, when he badly sprained his shoulder and battled through it. Or in 2009, when he played through plantar fasciitis in his foot. (Nobody knew how much pain he was in both of these times because it's not his nature to make a big deal of things like that.) Or the 2011 NFC Championship game, when the 49ers battered him, sacking him six times and hitting him twelve additional times. But Eli kept getting up. That's who he is, in a nutshell.

Another thing people don't see: the family man he is. And the charity work he does, for more charities than I can count, including mine, the Jay Fund, which helps families of children who have cancer. He won the NFL's Walter Payton Man of the Year award in 2016 in recognition of his good work. With everything he does, Eli cares deeply, and Eli puts in the work.

To the extent that we go down in football history together as a coach-quarterback tandem, I'm very honored by that. I remember, decades ago, the way my college coach Ben Schwartzwalder would talk about players he profoundly respected: He'd always say, *I'd be very proud to have this young man as my son.*

I have two sons and two daughters, and I couldn't be prouder of all of them. But that's how I feel about Eli.

———

Back in 2004, though, we were just at the beginning and had a long way to go. Everyone knows Eli struggled his rookie year. We were 5-4 when I made the switch from Kurt Warner to Eli, and we lost our next six games. We'd been in the division race with

Kurt, and with Eli we'd fallen out of it. It wasn't a popular decision among some of the veterans, and while I didn't care for some of the popping off I heard in the locker room, I understood their frustration. The media, too, was relentless: Here was the number one draft pick whose last name was Manning, but he had a completely different outward personality from his brother and he wasn't winning any games.

But in our building, we never wavered. Two moments from that season stood out and gave me a good feeling about where we were headed.

The first took place after one of the lowest points of the season: We'd just gotten blown out in Baltimore and Eli had struggled badly. It was our third lopsided loss in a row. The Ravens were an aggressive defense and they'd thrown every possible blitz at him, and it was more than he could handle. He was confused and he'd lost his poise. The defense had gotten in his head—and it was obvious to everyone.

Early the next day, he came into my office, and I took note: Most players try to avoid the head coach's office at all costs, but here was a rookie quarterback proactively coming in, in the worst of times. For most of the season, as a rookie and the backup, Eli had largely remained in the background. But now he was the starting quarterback who'd lost his first four games, and he felt compelled to say something.

He told me he'd played very poorly the day before. He acknowledged that he'd been rattled by the blitz and had lost his composure. And then I'll never forget what he told me next.

—*But Coach*, he said. *I know I can be the quarterback of the New York Giants. And I know we can win.*

He was extremely emotional—near tears. *That's* how passionate he was about being the player he knew he could be, the player we were counting on. That's Eli—and that's the guy most people on the outside don't see. No, they see the quiet, placid demeanor and don't really understand the fire at his core. But I've never been around a football player who wanted to be great more than Eli, or a player who's more passionate about winning.

As the season wound down, the losses continued to mount, but Eli's play improved. Then, in the last game of the season, we played the Dallas Cowboys, who were having a down season themselves in which they'd finish 6-10. We were depleted by injuries by that point, and in the Dallas game I had a hard time getting enough defensive linemen to dress. But we hung around that game, and with sixteen seconds left, we found ourselves down by three points, having driven the ball down to the Cowboys' 3-yard line. We had no time-outs, and we called a pass play—but one that gave Eli the option to audible to a run. This would've been risky: We had time for at least two passes, but a run would have made one more play very unlikely.

But Eli correctly sized up that the Cowboys didn't have enough men in the box, so he audibled to a draw play to Tiki Barber, who took it in for the game-winning touchdown. The crowd went wild, our players went wild, I took a baseball crow hop and did a huge fist pump. We'd been fighting to win a game for the last several months and we deserved that. More specifically, Eli had been working his tail off all year and continually had to face down sixty media members and explain why he wasn't yet his brother. *He* deserved that.

That audible call tells you everything you need to know about Eli: Think about the courage it took to call a running play, and how skewered by the press Eli would've been if the Cowboys had stopped Tiki. Our franchise quarterback, carrying the expectations of his last name, went winless in his rookie season and declined the chance to win the final game with his arm. But that's the thing about Eli: He doesn't care what anyone might think or say about him. He saw what he saw and he made the call he felt in his gut was right. And his trust in his instincts paid off.

That moment was a big confidence booster. So was much of the following year, when Eli really came into his own after we signed Plaxico Burress and got Amani Toomer back from injury. One moment sticks out that Giants fans will remember: With our record at 3-2, Denver came into town at 5-1 for a 4 p.m. game. The crowd had a special intensity that day; it was an early test to see if our strong start was for real and how we'd fare against a top team like Denver, who wound up making the AFC Championship game that year. Down by six points with 3:30 left, Eli led us on an 83-yard touchdown drive to win the game. Giants Stadium exploded, and so did our sideline, because everyone was thinking the same thing: *We have our quarterback.*

There were ups and downs after that: We won the division in 2005 but then fizzled in the playoffs after injuries decimated our team. In early 2006, Eli brought us back to win from a 24–7 fourth-quarter deficit in Philadelphia en route to a 6-2 start. But in late 2006, we went 2-6 down the stretch, and after a playoff loss to Philadelphia, the media wanted me fired and were ready to write off Eli. In 2007, Eli had two bad games in late-season losses against Washington and Minnesota, and the chorus of doubters was back. But Eli tuned them out like he always did, and in the playoffs he played the best football of his career to that point.

The Tampa Bay game: People forget we only managed three total yards in the first quarter and were down 7–0 against one of the league's best defenses, playing with a banged-up offensive line.

The Dallas game: They'd beaten us twice and had thirteen Pro Bowlers, an NFL record. They controlled much of the game in the first half with their huge line and punishing running game. And then our offense took over on our 29 with forty-seven seconds remaining in the half, and Eli marched us downfield for a game-tying touchdown, hitting Kevin Boss on a perfect touch pass down the sideline to set up our score. The touchdown took the air out of the building. We came out in the second half and outplayed them thoroughly, and moved on.

The Green Bay game, for the NFC Championship, will go down in football history. Eli on one side, Hall of Famer Brett Favre on the other. A wind chill temperature of minus twenty-four degrees at kickoff and getting colder with each passing minute, and Eli didn't flinch. He threw the ball around the yard like it was seventy-five degrees and he was playing in his childhood backyard in New Orleans. What he and Plaxico Burress did that day was a simple pitch-and-catch: Plaxico physically overmatched opposing cornerback Al Harris, basically manhandling him and getting separation that way, and Eli was on target with every throw.

Giants fans learned something about Eli that day.

The league learned something about Eli that day. He gave his best performance when we needed it most, something we'd all see again. Equally impressive to me is what it said about Eli's mentality: He'd blocked out the temperature just like he'd blocked out all the noise and negativity from day one. On that day, as ever, the only thing that mattered to him was winning the game.

———

And now here we are, in Arizona, with just one more game to win.

Eli's demeanor in the huddle is all business. Like our team, he has overcome a lot to get to this moment. Like our team, he has no doubt he deserves to be here.

But on our first set of downs, on two running plays, we gained only five yards. Faced with a third-and-five, we relied on our formula from our previous game in Green Bay: Eli to Plaxico. It was a square-in route, and we gained fourteen, moving the ball to our 42.

Plaxico was in the slot on the play, and at the top of his route there was contact with Randall Gay, the Patriots' five-eleven, 190-pound slot cornerback, which meant the six-six, 230-pound Plaxico had the advantage, and he created separation that way. Back in 2007, officials allowed a lot more contact between receivers and defensive backs than they do today. In most cases, the old interpretation of the rules benefited the defense, but the opposite was true in the case of Plaxico, who had long arms and was incredibly strong, and thrived on outmuscling defensive backs.

We were extremely grateful to have Plaxico out there. All year long, he had been dealing with a damaged tendon in his right ankle, meaning that his right foot had no stability. He had played all year while mostly not practicing. Then, the week of the Super Bowl, he slipped getting out of the shower and badly sprained his left knee. At the time, I wasn't terribly worried: I figured the knee would be good enough by Sunday. But as the week went on, it wasn't responding well, and a little more than two hours before the game, with the deadline to submit our list of inactive players looming, it was an open question whether he'd play or not.

I'd prepared for the possibility that he wouldn't play, but we would've been much worse off. Proof of that came less than a year later when our offense sputtered in our last several games after we'd lost him in late November. When a guy is such a big part of what you do, it's basically impossible to adjust on the fly to fully compensate for that loss. If Plaxico wasn't able to go, we would've changed our distribution of targets and featured the tight end more, but we would have been less than the best version of ourselves. On the Patriots' side, I have no doubt Bill Belichick would've adjusted his game plan quickly, likely bringing in extra support against the run and making it hard to achieve the run-pass balance we strive for.

But I was optimistic he'd play. Plaxico had battled through severe pain all year. And this was the Super Bowl.

Minutes before I had to submit my inactives, our great longtime trainer, Ronnie Barnes, took Plaxico out to the field to run him through a series of tests. He liked what they saw, at least enough. I was doing some last-minute preparation in my coach's room abutting the locker room when Ronnie poked his head in: *He's playing*, he told me, and then Ronnie left, because we both had lots to do. I breathed a huge sigh of relief.

As far as I was concerned, if Plaxico was playing, there would be no restrictions, and he would get every opportunity to make as big of a contribution as he had all year. Just having him out there was helpful, but as the game progressed, it became obvious how limited he was, and we had to scale back his role. His catch on our opening series was one of just two balls he caught all day. Everyone remembers his second catch.

The initial first down allowed us to settle into the game. After the previous two weeks, after all the pregame hype, we were finally doing what we came here to do: Play and win a football game.

———

The defense we were facing had been underrated all year, overshadowed by the Patriots' historic offense. But they weren't just good, they were excellent: fourth in the NFL in both points and yards allowed. Think about the stars and Hall of Famers who lined up across from us: Vince Wilfork, Richard Seymour, Adalius Thomas, Asante Samuel, Tedy Bruschi, Mike Vrabel, Rodney Harrison, Junior Seau. And they were coached by the best defensive coach in the history of the sport.

Ever since his days as the Giants' defensive coordinator, Belichick has always favored the 3-4 defense—having linebackers named Taylor, Banks, Carson, and Pepper Johnson will do that to any coach. His '07 Patriots defense lent itself to the 3-4: There was Wilfork occupying blockers in the middle, Seau and Vrabel as the classic middle linebackers, and Adalius Thomas as their edge rusher. But one of the things that makes Bill a great coach is his ability to adapt, and in his years with the Patriots,

Bill always tailored his defenses to the quality of his personnel and to the opponent on the other side.

He knew we wanted to establish the run, so he wanted to stop the run and show our blockers different fronts so that the defense wasn't predictable. On our first series, for our first ten plays on first and second downs, he threw a kitchen sink of fronts at us: On five of those plays, he used the base 3-4. On two plays, he used a 3-4 under, which makes it a four-man line. On three plays, he used three different versions of a sub package.

He mixed it up to keep us on our toes, and also to see how we'd react to those different fronts: If you've ever seen him on the sideline, you've noticed that he's always studying still photos. By using different fronts on the first drive, he was gathering information for subsequent drives.

Another hallmark of Belichick's defenses: He takes away the big play. Super Bowl XLII was no exception. In the secondary, he'll mix man and zone coverages while keeping three men deep who are responsible for keeping everything in front of them. He'll throw in some blitzes—on the first drive, he blitzed the Mike linebacker and the strong safety— but he's not going to do anything that leaves him susceptible to the big play. He is very confident in his personnel, as he should be, and he'd rather rely on his players to win individual matchups than bring more people than the offense can block while leaving himself vulnerable on the back end. In our Week 17 game, when we scored thirty-five points, we hit on some big plays, including a fifty-two-yard pass to Plaxico. Bill didn't want that to happen again.

Given this, our play calling on that first drive was modest: grind, grind, grind, with only one deep pass late in the drive. We wanted to establish a run-pass balance early on, and on that first drive, nine of our fifteen plays from scrimmage were running plays.

Run-pass balance and emphasizing the play-action pass were fundamental principles of our offense with the Giants and a point of agreement between me and our offensive coordinator, Kevin Gilbride, ever since he was my offensive coordinator in Jacksonville in the 1990s. The basic idea is that in any formation, alignment, or personnel grouping, and in any situation, we want to keep the defense guessing. Having a good run-pass balance is the *goal*—obviously, the game situation dictates the plays. But ideally, we want to be balanced and to keep our offense on schedule, because as long as the down and distance are manageable, we have confidence we'll be able to pick up first downs.

This was what we had in mind when we scripted our first fifteen plays. A note on *scripting* the opening plays, which is near universal in the NFL: It's not that we as coaches plan the first fifteen plays regardless of situation. Rather, we establish a hierarchy of the plays we want to run on first down, the plays we want to run when we need three to five yards, and the plays to run when we need seven to ten yards, and we work through that script in practice. The point is to get into a rhythm, to build confidence in what we're doing and to establish continuity between what we've practiced and what we're doing in the game.

On our next set of downs after our initial first down, we gained just four yards on our first two plays. Facing a third-and-six, we called a play for a guy who'd been stepping up big for us the past several weeks: Steve Smith. We liked the matchup in the slot between Steve and Randall Gay, and Steve ran a quick out for an eight-yard gain, putting us near midfield.

The emergence of Steve the past several weeks had been huge for us. Inactive for much of the season with shoulder and hamstring injuries, and after having missed eleven games, Steve came back in Week 15 against Washington, which, as fate would have it, is when we lost Jeremy Shockey for the year with a broken leg. The absence of Jeremy created a need for someone who could win matchups in the middle of the field, and Steve stepped up. His role increased week by week, and by the time the Super Bowl came around he was an integral part of our offense.

Steve was everything you'd want in a slot receiver: He was incredibly smooth, which meant that he created good separation out of his breaks because he didn't telegraph his direction with herky-jerky movements. And while he wasn't a blazer in the forty-yard dash, he was extremely quick. Add to that his intelligence and his feel for down and distance, and it's no stretch to say he was a budding star at the time of the Super Bowl. A couple years later, in 2009, at the age of twenty-four, Steve made the Pro Bowl and set a still-standing record for receptions for a Giant with 107. But then he suffered a devastating knee injury and was never able to get back to where he was. It makes me sad to think about, but it makes me realize how lucky we were to have Steve on our side in Super Bowl XLII. That third-and-six reception was a big play, and it wouldn't be Steve's last that night.

———

On our next set of downs, some running plays finally hit: Brandon Jacobs off left tackle for seven, and then Ahmad Bradshaw for two. On third-and-inches, from a short-yardage formation, we ran Ahmad behind Chris Snee and Kareem McKenzie, our most powerful run blockers, with the tight end lined up to that side. Ahmad hit a hole and ran through a shoulder-tackle attempt by a corner coming in from the perimeter. Then he put his hand on the ground to balance himself and got up under massive Patriots defensive end Ty Warren and, with the help of Kareem, drove Warren about six yards downfield, down to the Patriots' 29-yard line.

The sight of Ahmad driving back a man who outweighed him by ninety pounds was an emotional spark. Our fans loved it—they rose to their feet, and our whole sideline amped up. Ahmad loved it, too, turning toward our sideline and flailing his arms. We'd wanted to establish our physicality and win the battle at the line of scrimmage, and that play gave us a shot of confidence.

We faced a third-and-seven on our next set, and Eli found Steve again. They had blitzed a safety on Eli's blind side but he rolled right, and Steve found a soft spot in the zone for a nine-yard gain, moving us to the Patriots' 17. Again, Steve's ability to get open was on display. So was Eli's football intelligence and ability to move around to buy himself some time, which for much of his career was far better than anyone gave him credit for.

The next play, we lined up in the shotgun and took a shot at the end zone: Plaxico was double-covered but Eli gave him a chance to make a play on the ball, but the pass was broken up. Plaxico had been outcompeting defensive backs for us for years, so I could understand Eli's decision to throw to him. But on that play, looking back, Plaxico seemed compromised by his knee.

On the subsequent second-down play, we ran the ball and lost a yard, and on the third-and-eleven after that, with nothing open past the first-down marker, Eli threw a short pass across the middle to Steve for just a four-yard gain. It was a small play but, to me, a significant one: Eli *could* have pressed and forced something that wasn't there. Had he been any less confident, had he bought into the narrative that we were overmatched by the mighty Patriots, he might have. But he didn't.

Lawrence Tynes came in to try a thirty-two-yard field goal. Two weeks before, Lawrence had kicked a forty-seven-yarder on a frozen field in overtime to send us to the Super Bowl. This time, there was no such drama, and he knocked the ball down the middle to put us up 3–0.

We were disappointed we didn't get into the end zone, but we were happy with the lead. We were also happy with the length of the drive: sixteen plays that chewed up nearly ten minutes of clock, meaning Tom Brady wouldn't get the ball until the 4:52 mark of the first quarter.

This was our plan—similar to the plan we used

the last time I was on the field with Belichick during a Super Bowl, in Tampa in 1991. That day, the Giants held on to the ball for nearly forty-one minutes, limiting the Bills to fewer than twenty minutes of possession time and only nine drives. It's a classic blueprint for limiting an explosive offense, and Eli Manning and our offense did their part like they'd done everything else we'd asked for all postseason.

And then Tom Brady jogged onto the field.

Chapter Two

LAST YEAR IT WAS MY ASS

18-0. The highest-scoring team in the history of the game at the time. Tom Brady, the greatest quarterback in the history of the game. Randy Moss and Wes Welker, one of the greatest deep threats and one of the greatest slot receivers, both having terrific years. Pro Bowlers at left guard and right tackle.

None of this is hyperbole. Our defense had its hands full. There's a reason the Patriots averaged a then-record 36.8 points during the regular season—including 38 against us in Week 17.

Everything about that offense was top-notch. Moss and Welker were the best at what they did, and their skill sets complemented each other perfectly, with Moss taking the top off of defenses and Welker working underneath. Kevin Faulk was one of the best pass-catching and third-down backs in the league. Tight end Ben Watson's speed and receiving ability made him a mismatch against linebackers. Their offensive line had no weaknesses. Their running game might have been overshadowed by their historic passing game, but it was excellent. Laurence Maroney was big and fast and averaged 4.5 yards per carry in 2007.

We'd accomplished our goal on our first drive by keeping that offense off the field for the first ten minutes. But after we kicked off, it was Maroney—who was also their kick returner—who hurt us first. Our kickoff wasn't deep enough. They made some key blocks. We lost contain on the edge on the Patriots' left side, and Maroney darted to the outside and burst up the sideline. We knocked him out of bounds, but not before he got to the Patriots' 45-yard line.

With that one play, the Patriots were in position to undo everything positive we'd done on our first drive. By the numbers, when the average team starts a drive at their own 45-yard line, they can be expected to score about 2.5 points. Well, the 2007 Patriots were no average team—they averaged a staggering 3.2 points on *all* drives. During training camp every year, I have a lecture devoted to field position and expected points. Fans may not pay so much attention to special teams, but they scare the hell out of any coach, and I wanted to stress to the players that games—especially between evenly matched teams—are often won and lost on special teams.

Now this. Our offense did its job to keep that Pats' offense off the field, but now Brady and his guys were starting with a big advantage.

We stopped them on the first play: a slow screen that was blown up by our nose tackle, Barry Cofield, who knocked Tom Brady to the ground and threw off the play's timing. That first play was predictive, a sign of things to come, and I'll discuss it at length later. Right now, the Patriots had a second-and-ten.

They called a running play, which was somewhat against tendencies for the 2007 Patriots. On second-and-long in 2007, the Patriots ran the ball 26 percent of the time, which was third-least in the league: Why run when you can get bigger chunks of yardage with the pass, right? Well, Bill Belichick's teams, at heart, will always strive for balance. They'd passed the ball forty-eight times against us in Week 17, with success—Brady threw for 356 yards—but they likely anticipated this would be a different kind of game, one in which they needed to establish balance.

So that second-and-ten play was a run, a basic off-tackle play to the offensive left side, behind Pro Bowler Matt Light, and Maroney picked up 8.5

yards. That brought up third down and 1.5 yards to go, and again they ran Maroney behind Light, and picked up five yards. That gave them first-and-ten at our 42-yard line. They were in our territory, knocking on the door of field goal range.

After one set of downs, the Patriots were doing something we couldn't allow them to do: establishing the run, particularly on the offensive left side, where Light had a big size advantage over Osi Umenyiora. (Teams ran the ball more frequently to the left side against us: On the other side was Michael Strahan, one of the best run-stopping defensive ends in the history of the league.) One of the big questions coming into the game was whether we could stop the run to prevent the Patriots from being in favorable down-and-distance situations. If that offense had you on your heels, you were in trouble. Three plays into their first drive, we were in some trouble.

With a first-and-ten, having softened us with the run, the Patriots tried a pass, but we covered it well and nobody was open, and Brady essentially threw the ball away. On the next play, a second-and-ten, the Patriots lined up with nobody in the backfield and five receivers—including Randy Moss, Wes Welker, and Kevin Faulk on the offensive right side. With our attention focused on *those* guys on *that* side, Donté Stallworth, working on the *other* side, was able to find a soft spot in the zone for a seven-yard gain. That brought up a critical play: third-and-three from our 35-yard line.

A first down would put the Patriots in field goal range. But anything short of that would give them a tough decision of whether to punt, kick a field goal, or go for it.

On defense, we had been aggressive all year under our coordinator Steve Spagnuolo. So in this big spot, it was no surprise he decided to blitz, rushing our inside linebackers Kawika Mitchell and Antonio Pierce. It was a blitz we'd use often that night, with great success—but it wasn't successful this time. Brady recognized the pressure before the snap and changed his blocking scheme to account for it. Much of what makes number 12 the best ever to do it is between the ears, and this is a great example of how he outthought us. With that protection adjustment made, our blitz was thwarted, giving Brady enough time to spot the matchup he wanted: Wes Welker in the slot on the left side, working against our cornerback Kevin Dockery.

We'd signed Dockery before the '06 season as an undrafted free agent out of Mississippi State, and he'd made the team and carved out a role for himself due to his outstanding quickness and toughness. He'd gotten knocked down on draft boards because of his size—he was five foot eight—but his low center of gravity made him a good fit for the slot, where shiftiness and change of direction are key, and these qualities made Dockery our best matchup against the five-foot-nine Welker. But Welker was too quick, too sudden, too crafty—nobody in the NFL had much of a chance against him for years, and like many of those Patriots, he was having a career year in 2007. From the offensive left slot, Welker faked a shallow crossing route but then planted his foot on a dime and darted toward the left sideline, freeing himself by about five yards. It was an easy throw for Brady and an eight-yard gain for the Patriots. They now had a first-and-ten from our 27. They were rolling.

On the play after the next, they *almost* popped a big play on us: From the shotgun, they ran a half-back speed screen to Kevin Faulk to the offensive right side, which was the wide side of the field.

On the play, Randy Moss had lined up on the *other* side of the field, the left side, which was significant because we were double-teaming him, which removed a defender from the side the Patriots chose to attack. The Patriots guessed correctly that we'd do that; it was a smart design by their coordinator, Josh McDaniels, who was then only thirty-one years old but would soon become a head coach.

On the right side, they had two receivers split out, and if the receivers held their blocks, Faulk could catch the ball while running diagonally between them, where he would have a running start to get to the edge with a chance to turn it up to score. (Faulk was a great player, a smooth receiver with a nose for the first-down sticks: In the Super Bowl, he caught seven passes, five of which went for first downs.)

Faulk caught a perfect pass in stride and then burst upfield on a diagonal. The receivers made the necessary blocks. Faulk would have had a very good chance of scoring had not Sam Madison, who was on the edge being blocked by the much-bigger Jabar Gaffney, fought off Gaffney *just* enough to make a shoestring tackle on Faulk. The Patriots picked up eight yards on the play for a first down, but thanks to Sam's play—he was thirty-three years old and nearing the end of a great career—it wasn't a touchdown.

That *seemed* like a big play at the time—and it loomed larger after the next two plays when we forced two incomplete passes, bringing up a third-and-ten from our 17-yard line. This is a very advantageous situation for the defense: It's hard to throw the ball for ten or more yards when the field is so compressed. After giving up field position on the kickoff and surviving the speed screen to Faulk, it looked like our defense had stiffened at just the right time.

But no. On third down, they made a big play and we didn't.

The call was a seam route down the middle to Watson, the tight end, who was lined up on the offensive right side and was working against Antonio Pierce. Also lined up on that right side? Randy Moss—and his presence drew the attention of our safety. This meant that Antonio was one-on-one against Watson—and Watson had a height and speed advantage.

The thing about Antonio was that lots of guys had physical advantages over him. He wasn't the fastest guy, he wasn't the biggest guy, he wasn't the hardest hitter. And yet he was a great player, an absolutely indispensable part of the team. The reason? I've never seen a defensive player with a greater passion for the intellectual aspect of the game. He always wanted to understand things in more detail. He wanted to know the reasons *why*.

Without Antonio, we wouldn't have been in the Super Bowl, up 3–0 on the Patriots. Two weeks before in Green Bay, he made one of the best plays in the history of the Giants franchise: With the Packers leading 7–6 in the second quarter, they faced a third-and-eight from our 19-yard line and called a screen pass. It was one of those moments in a football game where a team calls the perfect play for the defense, perfectly lucky for them but perfectly unlucky for us. They outnumbered us on that side of the field and had a path to an easy touchdown—if not for Antonio. Single-handedly, he read the play perfectly and somehow split a wall of blockers to make the tackle. It was a superhuman effort, one that showed how anticipation and desire trump physical attributes any day of the week.

The Packers were forced to settle for a field goal, meaning the tackle alone was worth four points. The game went into overtime. It's no stretch to say that without that tackle, we'd have lost that game.

That's what Antonio was all about. I remember when I first met him, when we took him out to dinner after the 2004 season. He was a free agent who'd distinguished himself for Washington. When he started talking, it was a "wow" moment: The guy knew as much about *our* offensive personnel and schemes as we did. I'd never seen anything like it. We were trying to build something and knew immediately that a guy like that was a foundational piece.

Antonio was a guy who just *got it*—he *got* that football is played with your brain as much as your body, and that preparation during the week is gonna be rewarded on Sundays. His enthusiasm for gaining those little edges was infectious. Guys saw the work he put in and they came away inspired to do the same.

With his savvy, he was like a coach on the field:

Often, he could predict exactly what play was coming based on the other team's formation and tendencies. The value of that kind of thing doesn't show up on the stat sheet and isn't visible to anyone watching at home, but it's incalculable.

I remember how awful it was when Antonio suffered a neck injury in 2009 that ended his career. It was so sudden—a first opinion, a second opinion, and then he was done. All that film study, all those presnap adjustments he made to bail out our defense, all those conversations he had with his teammates—gone in the blink of an eye. Antonio's value can be summed up by what happened to our defense in '09 after he went down.

Now he's the linebackers coach with the Las Vegas Raiders after being the defensive coordinator at Arizona State University. That makes me smile: That man was born to coach defense.

All that said, fifteen years before, on the Patriots' first drive in Super Bowl XLII, having to run downfield with Ben Watson was a tough matchup for him. On the play, Antonio was expecting safety help, but with Randy Moss also lined up on that side of the field, the safety help never got there because we were so concerned about Moss.

Give Antonio credit—he stayed with Watson step for step all the way to the end zone. But in order to keep up with him, he turned his back to the quarterback. Tom Brady's pass was underthrown—whether this was intentional or not I don't know, but it worked to the Patriots' advantage: Watson came back for the ball, and Antonio wasn't looking, and they collided in the end zone. The pass fell incomplete but Antonio was flagged for pass interference, giving the Patriots a first-and-goal from the 1.

It was a huge play: Who wins or loses the game often hinges on a high-leverage play like this, even though it was in the first quarter. Two plays later, on the first play of the second quarter, the Patriots scored a touchdown on a Maroney run.

Patriots 7, Giants 3.

At this point, it was easy to imagine what most people watching the game were thinking: It had taken the Patriots a little while to get rolling, but after one quarter, the team that was supposed to win was winning—and their lead would only get bigger as the game went on.

On our sideline, though, we were disappointed but not disheartened. They had moved the ball on us, but we had confidence our offense could move the ball on them as well—based on the Week 17 game and also our first drive. After one round of possessions, it felt like we'd stood in the middle of the ring with them and traded blows. The score was in their favor, but we weren't intimidated.

———

Most NFL coaches wear a headset that covers only one ear, leaving the other ear free to communicate with people on the sideline. But I wear the one that covers both. The reason is that I prefer the balanced feel of it, but maybe it says something deeper about me: With everything I do, I want to be completely immersed in the task at hand, minimizing distractions as much as possible. If someone comes up to me to say something, or if I need to say something to the officials, I'll push the headset back on my head, but mostly it stays on all game. I can hear the crowd noise, but it's muted and in the background. What I need to hear is the feed from my coordinators. That's the priority.

There are three separate feeds: for offense, defense, and special teams, and I push a button to switch feeds. I don't call the plays and I seldom interfere, but I'm *involved*. On every play, a coach knows exactly the thing to watch that will determine whether the play is successful or not, and watching, processing, and figuring out what worked and what didn't takes up most of my mental energy. Between series, I debrief with the coordinators about what went right, what went wrong, and what needs to be done going forward. During games, there's no time to think about anything else.

Given that, during the actual game flow of Super Bowl XLII, I can't say there was a moment when I took it all in, or reflected on the sights and sounds. This means it wasn't until much later, when I saw the clip from one of the NFL Films highlight tapes, that I thought about my pregame conversation with Mike Carey and the officiating crew.

It was the same pregame conversation I've had hundreds of times during my twenty years of being an NFL head coach. You come out onto the field. The officials tell you that you can direct your time-outs to them. They tell you they'll let you know if anything out of the norm happens. They tell you not to worry about crossing the box of the 30-yard line if you need a time-out when the ball is at the end of the field. Then you have friendly small talk with them for a couple minutes.

That evening, the officials told me that I seemed upbeat. And they were right: I was at peace with the knowledge that we'd done everything we could to prepare, and I was excited to see how we'd perform.

Then one of the officials asked me how my face was—a reference to something a lot of people had been joking about: the frostbite on my face in Green Bay, from two weeks before. It had been minus twenty-four degrees with the wind chill, the third-coldest game in NFL history. During the second half, my face got redder and redder, until it was a deep beet-red shade, chapped at the cheekbones and nose. I didn't notice—the game demanded all of my focus and then some. But after we won, the frostbite took on a life of its own in the media. It became emblematic of our team's ability to overcome hardship and to persevere, no matter the circumstances.

And so, I joked with the officials, it was notable that everyone was talking about my *face*.

Last year, I said, *it was my ass*.

———

Flash back to December 24, 2006. We're playing the New Orleans Saints in a 1 p.m. game on Christmas Eve, but the temperature is a balmy-for-the-season fifty-two degrees. It's sunny and hope is in the air: Even though we've lost five of our last six games as injuries have decimated our team, a win at home gets us into the playoffs. It's likely to be the last home game of the season, so the fans are up for the game, hoping to send us off on a good note.

But things turn sour. We fall behind, and by the early fourth quarter, we're down 27–7, en route to a dreadful 30–7 loss. Throughout the fourth quarter, I'm later told, pockets of angry fans start chanting: *Fi-re Coughlin*, in the same melody as the *Let's go Yankees* chant. At the time, I don't hear them. There are many reasons I wear the double headset, after all.

The next week, we win at Washington to clinch a playoff berth, but then we lose in the first round at Philadelphia. We'd started off 6-2 but then went 2-7 in our final nine games, including the playoff loss. I could point out that down the stretch, we'd suffered an awful rash of injuries to guys like Michael Strahan and Amani Toomer, and lost close games to good teams that could have easily gone the other way. But the media narrative was set: Tom Coughlin, in his hard-driving, antiquated ways, had *lost his team*. He needed to get out of the Meadowlands on the next train out of Secaucus Junction.

The headlines after the playoff loss held nothing back:

New York *Daily News*: "Coughlin Must Go. Ax Can't Fall Fast Enough"

New York Post: "Coughlin Should Be Through with Little Blue"

New York Post again: "Keeping Coughlin Would Be a Big Blue Boo-Boo"

The Monday after we got eliminated, I went into the office to prepare for the off-season. I left work for the day and then pulled into my driveway at home. That's when I saw the cars of my son Tim and daughter Kate.

It was like walking into an intervention. They'd been reading everything in the papers for weeks. Unbeknownst to me, they'd been emailing back and forth with my wife about how much the writers were teeing off on me. The criticism went beyond football; it became personal, an indictment of my character, and a gang-up. The coverage had a nasty, mean-spirited edge, as if I'd done something to harm these people and they were exacting retribution.

During these weeks, I was mostly oblivious about what was being said in the papers. I'm so immersed in the day-to-day aspects of the job that I go through the season with blinders on—it's the same idea as wearing the double headset. But my family saw it and felt it. I'll never forget when my son looked at me with an expression of pain and concern, as if *he* were the father and I were the son.

—*Is it . . .* worth *it?* he asked me.

I was floored and had no idea what to say.

I'd always had a tense relationship with the media, but it wasn't something I'd spent any time thinking about. I'd get annoyed at the repetitive questions, and sure, I could have been more polite about not showing my annoyance, but it wasn't like I harbored strong negative feelings. I didn't read the papers or watch ESPN. Instead, I told Pat Hanlon, the Giants' great, longtime communications guy, to tell me only what I needed to know—which reporters were ripping our team, which to be careful with, which were fair—and nothing more.

But seeing my family this upset about how I

was being portrayed? That was a punch to the gut I didn't see coming. The hurt on *their* faces hurt *me*.

The next day, I had a meeting with John Mara and Jonathan Tisch to discuss my job status. There was only one year left on my contract. There's a perception out there that I was called on the carpet, and that I had to plead my case to keep my job, vowing to change my ways. But I never saw it that way. I had a feeling when I walked into that room that they didn't want to fire me. Rather, they were just looking for reassurance we were on the right path. And I provided that reassurance: I told them I still thought we had a very good team that was capable of competing for Super Bowls. I told them I still thought I was the right man for the job—and more importantly, that the *players* trusted I was the right man. After the meeting I got a two-year contract covering 2007 and '08, a customary move so I wouldn't be a potential lame-duck coach in '07.

That said, I did come out of that meeting vowing to make some changes. The first involved the toxic dynamic that had developed between the media and me. The situation had become untenable. We needed to clear the air.

To that end, Pat Hanlon arranged a series of one-on-one sit-downs with media members after the season. Pat's a person who everyone in the business respects, so he was the perfect go-between.

From my side, I had two basic questions: *What is it you don't like about me? What can I do to help you?*

Some writers answered honestly. Some squirmed and acted like they hadn't been ripping me when I knew they had. The best conversations were with the ones who were forthright. Neil Best from *Newsday* and Paul Schwartz of the *New York Post* were frank with me but not belligerent. They told me they had nothing against me personally, but that I sometimes came off as unnecessarily hostile and even demeaning.

I reflected on my demeanor during those press conferences. Do you remember what I was like? I'm leaning on the lectern, with my body rocking slightly with impatience, my fingers tapping the lectern's sides, itching for it to be over so I can get back to work. The way I looked at it, it's a feeling anyone who has ever worked any job can relate to. I'm in the middle of my workday, focused on a million things, and here I have to stop and answer questions— many of which are actually traps to get me to say something that can be taken out of context. It wasn't that I disliked any media members personally. It was just that answering their questions was never the thing I wanted to be doing at that moment, and my demeanor reflected that. I was impatient, and I sometimes couldn't help myself from snapping at provocative questions.

Sitting down with the writers helped defuse the tension. I realized they were people with jobs, just like I was. Neil, Paul, and some others convinced me it would be in everyone's best interests if I put a little more thought into giving the writers a few nuggets they could use. I was never going to be effusive, but there was certainly some middle ground to be found, and that seemed reasonable to me. And if I was ever disrespectful to them or made their jobs harder when I didn't have to, I resolved to correct that.

With a clean slate established, the press and I came a long way during the '07 season. By Media Day of the Super Bowl, I was calling the local reporters by their first names. On that day, I actually *enjoyed* being peppered with questions.

But I don't want to overstate this whole thing. I didn't change *that* much, nor in any fundamental way. And it certainly wasn't sunshine and rainbows between the press and me from that point forward. In 2010, after we missed the playoffs despite going 10-6, I gave a postgame speech to my team in the locker room where I told them our critics could "kiss my ass," and the speech was caught on camera and circulated on social media. The following year, after we hit a rough patch late in the season, a lot of journalists were calling for my head, again. Then we went on a run and won the Super Bowl, again.

The fact is, I was never a sports figure who made

it easy for the media to wrap their arms around me. I wasn't gonna be the guy to warm them up with funny stories or pearls of folksy wisdom. I was never gonna call this or that writer late at night to give them off-the-record scoops. I was never gonna use the press to motivate my players, violating what to me is a sacred code that a football team is a family and that problems stay within the family.

Some people in sports care a lot about what the media says about them. They're motivated, in part, by the adulation, needing the writers to turn them into living legends. But that was never me. I never viewed myself as a genius or a guru of human psychology. I viewed myself as a worker, a guy devoted to the fundamentals of the game itself who wanted to succeed in the NFL because it was the pinnacle of the profession, and not because it would make me famous.

If anything, I actively *didn't* want the press to pump up my ego, because humility is something I've always valued, going back to my upbringing as an altar boy in the Catholic Church. *Deeds, not words. The last shall be first*—I believe in all of those values with every fiber of my being. Whatever success I had, I've always found that being humble put me in the right frame of mind to achieve it. The moment you start thinking that you're bigger than the game is the moment the game lays you low. After big wins,

I'd always repeat the mantra in the locker room: *Humble in victory, proud in defeat.* There's always another game. Pausing to reflect on how great you are puts you at a disadvantage.

I realize these are meat-and-potatoes values. They don't lend themselves to superlatives, and they're not the stuff of sports mythology. But I never cared. I didn't revere the stories *surrounding* the game—I revered the game itself. Call me naive, but my love for the sport is pure. Love for team, love for climbing the mountain together. *That's* what I live for. I was watching the Stanley Cup Finals the other night, and I got chills watching the Tampa Bay Lightning jumping all over each other. That moment is what it's about for me—and not the praise that follows.

This kept me at an arm's distance from the media. Perhaps at points it had kept me at a distance from the fans as well. I didn't have the type of personality for the media to convey to them in the most compelling terms. But looking back, I think the fans came to embrace me *because* of this quality. When people think of New York, they think of the glamour and celebrity, but that's actually a small fraction of what defines the area. What makes the city run is the nurse on the subway at 4 a.m. about to put in a double shift. Or the people cleaning the office buildings. Or the cops and the firefighters. After the 9/11 attacks, I was still the coach at Jacksonville, and I was extremely honored to wear the NYPD and FDNY hats. In my mind, New York is all about people doing the *work*. And looking back, I'd like to think I formed a special connection with New Yorkers because of the work I put in.

But going into the 2007 season? I had a lot of work to do.

———

Improving my relationship with the press was one thing I had to work on. Improving my relationship with the players was another.

Let me tell you a story about how I was raised in the game: My freshman year at Syracuse, I was practicing under my coach, Ben Schwartzwalder, an old-fashioned guy who preached the virtues of physical toughness, running summer sessions consisting of two practices that were three hours each—we practiced until he got tired, we'd always joke. During a scrimmage that spring, I caught a screen pass and was supposed to cut to the outside, where the play was designed. But I cut *inside* instead, and after I did, a defender I didn't see hit my knee, injuring my MCL.

I was lying on the grass in pain when Coach Schwartzwalder came over. Some twenty years before that moment, he had volunteered for service in World War II as a paratrooper. Back then he was thirty-two years old, one of the oldest paratroopers ever, and he dropped behind enemy lines on D-Day. On the practice field at Syracuse, he looked down at his injured freshman back.

—*That'll teach you to cut inside on the screen pass,* he said in a matter-of-fact voice.

Then he moved the scrimmage downfield a few yards, away from me, and resumed practice. The MCL injury was just a sprain, and I came back in two weeks and had a good spring game on my way to becoming a key part of the team. And Coach Schwartzwalder became one of my coaching idols.

All of that goes to say that by 2007, there was a generational gap that existed between me and the players. I was sixty at the time. Most of them were nearly four decades younger.

I came to New York with a reputation that preceded me from my days with the expansion Jacksonville Jaguars. Our very first training camp in 1996 was in Stevens Point, Wisconsin. "Camp Coughlin," the writers called it, and it became known as kind of a latter-day Junction Boys (Bear Bryant's famously ruthless summer camp at Texas A&M) for how physically demanding it was. The irony is that we went north to Wisconsin for a cooler climate, but a brutal heat wave hit and the temperature was 104 degrees the entire first week. I'll never forget the sound of guys' feet squishing in their cleats because so much sweat had pooled under their feet.

That camp was something I felt I needed to do to set a tone with a brand-new organization. I was well aware that as an authority figure, you can always start off tough and ease off, but you can't do the opposite. The situation in Jacksonville was unique: The first ten players on our roster hadn't been on an NFL team the year before, and the rest of the team consisted mostly of guys other teams didn't want. My office the first two years was in a trailer next to our under-construction stadium. We were under-manned in just about every way. I knew the only way we wouldn't get blown out in every game was if we outworked people and were physically tougher than them.

I was right. In our first year we went 4-12, but we were competitive; we put a thermometer behind the opponent's bench during home games to remind them how hot it was. The next season, with that foundation of toughness in place, we added some free agents, made the playoffs at 9-7, and then went on a run to the AFC Championship game.

By the time I got to the Giants, the image of me from that first camp in Jacksonville had stuck. I was a drill sergeant, "Colonel Coughlin." While I did nothing to downplay that, the perception was exaggerated and off the mark. I'm a practical person, and everything I did, I did for the purpose of winning games and making my players better as both athletes and human beings. In reality, my practices were always very *short*—maybe one hour and forty minutes, though we kept a brisk pace and went from drill to drill without wasting time. Michael Strahan has actually been quoted as saying that physically, my practices were the *least* demanding of any coach he'd had; what distinguished them was the focus I expected of players.

But the die was cast, I was put into a box, and several rules I had for my teams fed into that portrayal. The most famous was "Coughlin Time," which said everyone had to be at meetings five minutes before the appointed time. As I saw it, this was a symbolic but significant rule: It was a way for our guys to show that they were committed to doing just a little bit extra, and doing so as a unit. (A favorite expression of mine is "There's no traffic on the extra mile.")

Other rules—during meetings: hats off, sit up straight, feet flat on the floor, make eye contact with the speaker—came from a similar desire to establish discipline and buy-in. These weren't just arbitrary ways for me to wield my power; they *meant* something. We're professionals, people *at work*. Many of these guys will work in offices after their careers end, and the lessons they learn will apply for the rest of their lives. I took very seriously that I was a formative influence on my players just as my coaches were on me.

I make no apologies for believing in discipline and structure. It's how I was raised growing up in a house with ten people, including my grandparents and six siblings. Structure was the only way things could work. You got up every day at a certain time, you came home at a certain time, you stopped making noise at a certain time so your grandparents could sleep, and you went to bed at a certain time. I went to a Catholic school and was an altar boy at church. An appreciation for discipline and structure is embedded in my religious beliefs. This is the environment that formed me—and I believe that it *worked*. I'm proud of who I became and what I accomplished, and I want to pass those values on.

My upbringing is probably why I gravitated to football the most of all sports. Football rewards discipline and structure and punishes the lack of either. If each of the eleven guys does his job to the best of his ability, the play will work. But if one guy takes a slightly false step, or if one guy's hand technique is sloppy, at best it ruins the play, and at worst people get hurt.

People tend not to like when an authority figure makes them uncomfortable, but guess what? Football is a tough game, and the teams that succeed are the ones that are comfortable being uncomfortable. That was what I was trying to instill during that first training camp in Jacksonville.

But by 2007, it was clear that something had been lost in translation. The perception was that I was a relic of a bygone era and was being tuned out by the players. That narrative was way overblown, but I still had to acknowledge that my communication with the players needed improvement.

I'd sense it when I'd walk past players in the facility and they'd look down, or do anything to avoid eye contact with me. Or when I'd give a talk to the team about the importance of togetherness, or responsibility, or leadership, or doing the right thing—and then hear them come out of the meeting room grumbling about me. In my mind I was trying to inspire them, but they were taking it as if I was browbeating them.

One day during the off-season before the '07 season, I had a light bulb moment. It came via an offhand comment from Charles Way, our director of player development and one of the most decent, intelligent men I've ever worked with, who'd been a very good football player for the Giants in the 1990s. *Coach,* he said to me, *you really ought to let the players see you like you are with your grandkids.*

That comment hit me like a ton of bricks. I thought about a scene that would frequently transpire after practice: My daughter Kate and her husband, Chris Snee, would bring their kids, and while the players were in the locker room, I'd goof around with them on the field, wrestling and throwing a football around. Charles saw that version of me. But the players didn't.

The version they saw of me was the coach I'd disciplined myself to become over decades in the profession. When I was around my players, *everything* was about the task at hand. Everything was serious and no time was wasted. In my mind, we were maximizing our chances of winning. But there was a cost: The players didn't know there was a human being underneath all of that. Charles was saying that there was value to showing them that person. That I had things beyond football that I loved and cared about, like the players did. That I had a soft side, even—something becoming a grandfather had put me more in touch with.

Charles's comment compelled me to show those sides of myself a little more with my players. But really, I had been evolving in this direction anyway. I was always interested in learning and getting better, and during the off-seasons I'd devour books on leaders like FDR or Eisenhower or Churchill, looking for lessons I could apply to my profession. Toward the late 1990s, I started reading books by, and about, John Wooden, and a lot of his wisdom jumped out at me. His teachings had an almost biblical application to what I'd experienced in coaching.

Wooden stressed that wins or losses usually reside in the preparation, long before the game actually starts. That big plays in games result from the accumulation of little details in practice nobody sees. That a person's competitive greatness doesn't exist in isolation—rather, it's part of excellence of character that also includes friendship, loyalty, and cooperation.

Over the next several years I talked to Coach Wooden several times and got to know him. Then, a few years before his 2010 death, when the NFL team meetings were in Southern California, I went to Coach Wooden's home and was privileged to have three hours of his time.

He was in his nineties by then, in a wheelchair, but age didn't diminish his eminence. He wore a light blue sweater, which of course put me in mind of UCLA. He was a warm and wonderful man, and those three hours went by so fast as he filled the time with stories about Kareem Abdul-Jabbar and Bill Walton. I was riveted.

He believed that as human beings we can never be perfect—but that shouldn't stop us from striving for perfection. He admired traditional disciplinarians like Vince Lombardi and even Bobby Knight, but he set himself apart from their methods; Wooden never even said the word "win" to his team, believing that doing so detracted from the message that the joy was in the preparation, not the result. One major thing I took from him was a change he made later in his life to his famous "Pyramid of Success," a set of philosophical building blocks for succeeding at sports and life. During Wooden's coaching career, at the top of the pyramid was "Competitive Greatness." But when he got older, he realized there was something even more important than competitive greatness: love.

I took that to heart. There was more to life than competitive greatness, and there was more to coaching a sports team than competitive greatness. Four years after the '07 game, in my Saturday night speech on the eve of the 2011 Super Bowl, I told my players that I was man enough to tell them that I loved them. That emotional mindfulness started in the changes I resolved to make before the '07 season.

———

But don't blow this "kinder, gentler Tom Coughlin" thing out of proportion. Similar to how I improved my relationship with the writers, this was a tweak around the edges, not a wholesale change. But it was important.

The first sign that things would be a little different in 2007 was during training camp at the State University at Albany. It was during the depths of the dog days, when everything becomes a grind, and guys are worn out mentally and physically. One evening, the players walked into a meeting, playbooks in hand, and sat down. We reviewed some items on the PowerPoint until one slide surprised them: *We're going bowling!*

Raucous cheers rang out. It was only one evening, sure, but the gesture was important. It signaled to them that I'd heard, through various channels, their feedback about me, and I was willing to give a little bit to make the relationship better.

We went to a nearby alley and had a great night. Nobody threw more gutter balls than me; nobody got made fun of more than me. When you take people out of the setting you normally see them in, you learn things about them—like that David Tyree and Kareem McKenzie were serious bowlers who owned their own balls. Most of the guys were dropping the ball from their waists when they rolled it— I thought they would break the floor—and I tried to have proper technique by bending more and rolling it quietly. Then I woke up the next day and could hardly walk, and everyone else was fine—and they made fun of me for *that*.

There were other instances early on like that— little, humanizing moments where we saw each other outside of the normal daily grind, which brought us closer together and allowed the players to see me as more than a guy barking orders. During minicamp in June, we had a casino night, where we brought in an outside company, which was another idea from Charles Way. One Saturday early in the season, we had a family fun day. When practice was over, everyone's families came onto the field, where activities were set up for the kids. Meeting the people behind the players gave me a whole new appreciation for these guys. I remember seeing Brandon Jacobs's in-laws, who he was extremely close to, and talking a lot to Olivia Manning. I'd known Archie for years and knew he was a great father, but talking to Olivia gave me a whole new appreciation for how Eli and Peyton turned out the way they did. A bunch of little kids were running around—my grandkids, the players' kids—and if that doesn't help break the ice, I don't know what will. It was a day I thought back on when I was in our hotel in Arizona, watching everyone's kids play in the pool outside my room.

But far and away, the most important thing I did as far as relating to the players in '07 was creating the leadership council. This was a group of veterans from every position group who had a say in matters like curfew and schedules. They filtered my message to the guys in their position groups, and vice versa.

Rule number one of the council was that it was a safe space: Anything a player said to me during those meetings was fair game and not something I would hold against them. Honesty was encouraged. We sat in a circle in chairs, as opposed to me standing and addressing them while they sat, which itself sent a message of collaboration.

Getting these guys into a small group allowed me to get to know them better. It also brought our team closer together by mixing guys from the offense, defense, and special teams, as well as each of the positional groups within those units. A football team is a company, and different units on the team are like different parts of the company, and often there's not much communication between them. But the leadership council cut through that, mixing guys with different personalities and all kinds of life experience.

There was Michael Strahan, a military brat who'd spent a lot of his childhood on an Army base in Germany. Offensive linemen like Shaun O'Hara and Richie Seubert and Dave Diehl, guys who are good at busting chops and just as good at getting their chops busted. Chris Snee, my son-in-law, who's quiet, serious, and smart. Antonio Pierce, the best student of the game I've ever been around. Jeremy Shockey, who left his wild-man persona outside the room for these meetings and contributed valuable insight. Sam Madison, an old pro with guile who's now a defensive backs coach for the Miami Dolphins. Corey Webster, who was sometimes quiet, but was quick-witted and a good friend to many guys on the team. Brandon Jacobs, loud, outgoing, passionate, and as loyal as the day is long. Jeff Feagles, a laid-back punter, quick with a smile, by then a forty-one-year-old whose career had begun in 1988. Eli, quiet but with a dry wit, and always something up his sleeve. Osi Umenyiora, who'd grown up in Nigeria and London and had the intelligence and confidence to navigate any social situation. Mathias Kiwanuka, another thoughtful, quiet guy off the field who flipped a switch between the lines and became a ferocious competitor. Amani Toomer, who had worked hard that year to get back from a serious knee injury and who, in the twilight of his career, was committed to doing whatever it took to win a championship.

The council created a sense of accountability by deputizing the veterans to be extensions of the coach. It's easy enough for a player to think *Screw this guy* when it comes to a coach. It's a lot harder to have that attitude toward Michael Strahan. And the gesture of giving the guys a say went a long way. It wasn't a democracy, exactly, but if there was a time that the council and I diverged on what was best, I can't remember it.

A good example of this was in the days leading up to the Super Bowl, when I asked the guys what they had in mind for curfew. Antonio Pierce then asked me: What did *I* have in mind?

So I broke down my plan: 1 a.m. Monday night, and then we'd taper it down day by day—12:30 on Tuesday, then 12, then 11:30, then Friday night at 11.

I asked him and the rest of the council: *What do you guys think?*

Antonio looked around the room. Everyone nodded.

That sounds good to us, he said, and that was that.

It was emblematic of how far we'd come: The players and the coach they'd supposedly tuned out were on the same page, focused on the objective ahead. The team the media had wanted to break up was in the Super Bowl.

Given all that, a 7–3 deficit with three quarters to play didn't seem so daunting.

Chapter Three

THE WAR HERO WHO HELPED GET US HERE

Of course, understanding and respect between players and coaches only goes so far. Ultimately, you have to win. And during the first two weeks of the 2007 season, we didn't win.

In Dallas on opening night, we lost 45–35, having given up huge play after huge play. The following week, in our home opener against Green Bay, we had a 10–7 halftime lead but then got outscored 28–3 in the second half to lose 35–13, a sudden blowout. It was a hot, humid day, and it felt like a daze: *How did that just happen?*

Two games in and we were already behind the eight ball. I'd just hired a new defensive coordinator, Steve Spagnuolo, and our defense had given up eighty points in our first two games. I can't imagine many people walking out of Giants Stadium that day thought highly of the 2007 Giants' chances. I didn't pay attention to what the papers said, but I doubt they were optimistic about my continued employment prospects.

Yet we never stopped believing in ourselves. And six days later, on the Saturday night before our next game in Washington, we were privileged to meet a very special person. That night, in our team hotel, Col. Greg Gadson stood before our team and embodied the values I'm constantly trying to stress to my team: discipline, toughness, service to others, sacrifice to a cause greater than oneself. After we met Greg Gadson, we were a different team.

Greg had been a linebacker on the Army football teams in the 1980s, where he played with our wide receivers coach, Mike Sullivan. They went their separate ways after they graduated, but in 2007, Greg called a bunch of his former teammates, including Mike, with big news: He was headed to Iraq, where he'd command a four-hundred-man unit.

During his deployment, on May 7, 2007, Greg was riding in an armored vehicle; he happened to be heading home from a memorial service for fellow soldiers who'd lost their lives. That day, on a road just outside of Baghdad, an improvised explosive device detonated, and the force of the explosion threw Greg out of the vehicle. When the medic finally got to him, he had no pulse and no blood pressure.

But his fellow soldiers never gave up on him, and one of the scattered memories he has from that day is of his unit members pleading with him to cling to life. He remembers the helicopters flying in to try to save him. The next thing he remembers was waking up in Germany, where he underwent multiple surgeries, and then being taken to Walter Reed Army Medical Center in Washington, DC. Both of his legs were amputated.

Four months later, Greg and Mike connected again. Mike would be coming to the DC area to play Washington for our Week 3 game. Mike put Greg and me in touch on the phone, and I was so impressed with him after speaking with him that I invited him to say a few words to the team on the Saturday night before our game. I remember meeting Greg for the first time and being struck by the purposeful look in his eyes. It's a look that tells you that Greg is made of different stuff than the rest of us. He was in a wheelchair but was a solidly built man who radiated strength.

In our hotel meeting room, when he told his story to our team, he had no notes; he just started talking. His presence—and everything he'd been through, and the fact that there wasn't an ounce of *woe is me* in him—was captivating. The guys sat there in rapt attention, never taking their eyes off him.

He talked about playing for each other: It was his fellow soldiers, after all, who'd saved his life. He talked about how the bond of any group is forged through difficulty, and how nothing worthwhile is achieved without struggle. He talked about how sports is a meaningful diversion for the soldiers overseas. He talked about how desperately he wanted to get back to his unit in Iraq.

When he was finished, you could've heard a pin drop in that room. For what seemed like minutes, nobody said anything. Everyone was just taking in what we'd heard. Then, everyone in the room stood up to give Greg a standing ovation. After that, one by one, the guys went up to him and thanked him. People were visibly emotional at what they'd just heard; I remember walking by hours later and seeing Plaxico Burress sitting at a table with Greg. If communication had ever been a problem between me and the players, well, Greg didn't have that problem. This guy knew how to cut to the core. He'd be on our sideline against Washington the next day, just like he'd be on our sideline for many games, including Super Bowl XLII.

This meant a lot to me, because I've always had great respect for our armed forces and the sacrifices they make. In fact, my hometown of Waterloo, New York, is considered the birthplace of Memorial Day after the townspeople commemorated soldiers who'd died in the Civil War in 1866. Greg's presence was a tremendous honor, and I took many lessons out of his speech. One in particular that stuck with me was a story, basically a parable, about a soldier who went on patrol in a violent section of Baghdad but didn't have to fire his weapon. When the soldier got back to the base, he was relieved his assignment was over and he didn't bother cleaning his weapon. Greg zeroed in on this: It's human nature to skip the meticulous details involved in preparation. To not clean the gun—or in our world, to skip just that little bit of extra preparation or study of the opponent. But human nature gets you beat every time; failing to prepare is dangerous. The soldier who stays alive is the one who cleans his gun. The NFL team that wins is the one that prepares just a little bit more. The team that's a little more comfortable being uncomfortable.

The following day against Washington, we were uncomfortable; we had fallen behind 17–3 by halftime. At that point, imagine the odds you could have gotten for us to win the game. Imagine the odds that I would've kept my job. Imagine the odds that we would've won the Super Bowl.

But nobody knew how tough we were. We'd show it time and again for the rest of the season. And it started in the second half of that game against Washington, with Col. Greg's words fresh in our minds.

Our defense clamped down, and we battled back to take a 24–17 lead. Then, Washington drove the ball to our 1-yard line, setting up a first-and-goal. It seemed impossible that we could keep them out of the end zone, but our defense put together an incredible goal-line stand that preserved the victory and saved our season. That win, and that goal-line stand, showed something that people would later learn about the 2007 Giants: We were at our best when our backs were against the wall. And it taught us that we were mentally tough enough, and we could accomplish amazing things.

I have no doubt our guys drew strength from Greg's words from the night before. After the game, in FedEx Field's cramped, dingy locker room, Greg came down and celebrated with our team, with guys slapping him on the back. To our great honor, he was one of us now.

We won five straight after that to go to 6-2. With Col. Greg by our side, we'd fight through all of it.

That's not to say there weren't more punches to the gut. Oh, there were plenty. That's football, after all.

In Week 12, Eli threw four interceptions—three were returned for touchdowns—in a 41–17 blow-out loss to the Vikings at home. All the negativity that people seemed to like to heap on Eli started up again.

Then, three weeks later, after a couple of hard-fought wins on the road, we came back home with a 9-5 record and a chance to clinch a playoff berth against a 6-7 Washington team that was starting its backup quarterback. It was a Sunday night game with midthirties temperatures, and our crowd was ready for the moment. But we came out flat and laid an egg, falling behind 13–0 and never getting back into the game in a 22–10 loss, during which we also lost Jeremy Shockey for the season with a broken leg.

To have played like that, with everything that was at stake, was incredibly disappointing. The next morning, when I walked into our locker room, I could feel the players' disappointment, as well as their fear. They thought I was about to go ballistic on them.

But here's something I learned from coaching in New York: After a game like that, the criticism from the New York media is absolutely merciless. You'll be down, and you'll get kicked, and then you'll get stomped. I knew that would happen, and that I didn't need to make them feel any worse. That morning, my speech to the team ahead of this critical week was short.

—*Gentlemen, we have two games left; we only need to*

win one to make the playoffs, I told them. My tone was unemotional, completely matter-of-fact.

—*I suggest we go into Buffalo and win, because otherwise we'll have to beat the undefeated Patriots.*

And then I walked out.

With that, the page was turned. When we came back into the facility on Wednesday after a day off, our focus was 100 percent on the Bills.

That Sunday, in Buffalo, the weather was awful, again. It might have been the worst-weather game I'd ever been a part of. Any bad condition you can think of—rain, sleet, snow, high winds—came off of Lake Erie that day, and for the second straight week we got off to a horrible start, falling behind 14–0 in the first quarter. But we clawed back into the game and then took the lead for good when Kawika Mitchell, a smart, hard-nosed linebacker who was a key free-agent addition that season, returned an interception for a touchdown. The clincher was Ahmad Bradshaw's eighty-eight-yard touchdown run late in the fourth quarter, which let people know two things: one, that we had an explosive rookie home run threat to pair in the backfield with Brandon Jacobs; and two, that we were a resilient team.

We were going to the playoffs.

But first there was a big game to play: New England would come into Giants Stadium six days after our Buffalo win for a Saturday night game. The question that would dominate the headlines for the next few days was asked immediately after the Buffalo game—and frankly, given what we'd just accomplished, it pissed me off to have to address it then: *Are you going to play your starters or rest them for the playoffs?*

I deflected the questions in the moment, but later, I thought about what I'd do. I've found that in my life, I'm at my best when things are at their most simplified. Fortunately, this situation seemed straightforward to me: We had an undefeated team trying to make NFL history, and I was a guy raised to respect the value of competition. We were the New York Giants, one of the flagship franchises of the NFL, a league whose popularity was built upon the idea of competition, ever since Wellington Mara convinced his fellow owners that revenue sharing would help all the franchises by ensuring competitive balance. It became very clear to me: There was no way I would allow the history books to say that the proud New York Giants organization stepped out of the way so the Patriots could go undefeated. Doing so would've been an insult to the history of the NFL and the history of the Giants. It would've been an insult to our fans. It would've been an insult to New York City, the greatest city in the world. It also would've been an insult to Bill Belichick and his team: If the Patriots were about to go 16-0, we weren't going to attach an asterisk to it.

I gave the players Monday off and then addressed them on Tuesday. I told them that as competitors, as *the New York Giants*, we would never let it be said that we didn't put our best foot forward. They accepted the challenge.

On game night, it was forty-four degrees, chilly but not too cold, and the crowd had a festive holiday energy for a game that took place between Christmas and New Year's. We exchanged touchdowns with the Patriots, and the lead swung back and forth. It was our last home game of the season, everyone knew. The year before, our last home game had been that dismal showing against the Saints, when the fans chanted "Fire Coughlin." But the energy in the building one year later was 180 degrees different. Our fans were fully behind us, and as we battled the Patriots, our fans were excited to learn that we could go toe-to-toe with the purported greatest team of all time.

The Patriots pulled away in the fourth quarter—we didn't put enough pressure on Tom Brady, and we let Randy Moss get behind us—and they completed their 16-0 season with a 38–35 win. There's no such thing as a good loss, and two of our starters, Shaun O'Hara and Kawika Mitchell, got injured that night and would miss our first playoff game. But we had proven something to ourselves, and were excited to keep playing.

The next morning, I came into my office early to start preparing for the playoffs. Then I saw the red light flashing on my phone, indicating I had a message.

It was John Madden. The football immortal who coached the storied Raiders teams of the 1970s, won a Super Bowl, and was enshrined in the Hall of Fame. The man who embodied everything great about football, who enjoyed his life in football like no other, and whose passing in 2021 would leave a hole in the heart of the sport. The man who broadcasted, with so much passion, all of those classic Giants games, including in the '90 season, when Bill Belichick and I won a Super Bowl together as assistant coaches.

The message he left gives me chills to this day.

He said he wanted to congratulate me for the great effort the night before—*not good, but great*, he said. He said the effort we showed was one of the best things to happen in the NFL in the past ten years. He said there's only one way to play this game, and that's to play to win. He said there'd been too much talk about resting our starters: *That's not sports and that's not competition.* He said he was emotional, and I could hear him choking up while he spoke.

He said, *I'm just so proud.*

The reason I would never consider giving less than our best in an NFL game, let alone one of historic significance, is because competition is sacred to me. I define myself as someone who embraces challenges. I'm wired like that. If you tell me I can't do something, I'm gonna come back at you with my very best.

By the time of the 2007 playoffs, our team was the same way. We had a chip on our shoulder. We'd been left for dead repeatedly, but here we were. Nobody gave us much of a chance, but that was fine with us.

Tell us we can't do something.

The Fox analysts just didn't like us, I guess. The first of four straight games they picked us to lose was our first-round matchup at Tampa Bay. The Bucs' coach was Jon Gruden, a proven Super Bowl winner. They had the second-ranked defense in the NFL by yards and were quarterbacked by Jeff Garcia, a crafty veteran who'd knocked us out of the playoffs the year before while playing for the Eagles. As for us, we were widely considered the worst team in the playoffs.

We fell behind 7–0 on that tough defense and our first three drives netted minus two yards. Since I got to the Giants, we'd lost our only two playoff games, and this was shaping up no better.

But then Eli led us on a touchdown drive to tie the game. From the beginning of that series forward, he went 18-for-23 with two touchdowns—and no interceptions or sacks. From that point forward, he became the best quarterback in the 2007 playoffs, just like we became the best team. Nobody saw either thing coming.

We eventually went up 24–7 before the Bucs scored a late touchdown to make the score look less lopsided. We won 24–14. Off to Dallas.

Tell us we can't do something.

Sunday morning, hours before our game against the Cowboys, I heard a report saying Jerry Jones had put two tickets on each of his players' locker stools to the NFC Championship game, which would have been played in Dallas if they'd won. He had some reason to be confident, I suppose. His Cowboys were the number one seed at 13-3. They'd beaten us twice in games where we couldn't stop their offense. They had thirteen Pro Bowlers.

I didn't make a big deal about the tickets. But I made sure my players knew.

We scored early on an Amani Toomer touchdown, but then the Cowboys took control for most of the rest of the half. They had a huge offensive line and a physical running back in Marion Barber, and they ground us down and controlled the clock, scoring on their second and third drives—including a Barber touchdown that put them up 14–7 with a minute to go in the half. At that point, they had thoroughly outplayed us. We hadn't stopped them in our previous two meetings and we weren't stopping them now.

With forty-seven seconds left in the first half, we took possession—and Eli led us on a touchdown drive that nobody except us saw coming. The key play was a third-down completion to Kevin Boss for nineteen yards that set us up for the score, a pass Eli lofted over the arm of a linebacker into tight coverage. It was one of those passes where anything less than a perfect pass doesn't get the job done. We'd see similar throws from Eli in the future.

That touchdown—a short pass to Amani Toomer—completely took the air out of Texas Stadium. It flipped the script: Up until that drive, the Cowboys had had an edge on us. But in the second half, they didn't seem like the version we'd seen all year, the 13-3 juggernaut and favorite to win the NFC. They were something less than their best. It felt like we'd absorbed their best punches for nearly two and a half games—and the fact that we were still standing left them exhausted. Now it was our turn to land some punches.

We took a 21–17 lead early in the fourth quarter, and then clung to it. The tension in the semi-indoor building escalated. And on the Cowboys' final drive, their last chance to win, R. W. McQuarters intercepted a pass in the end zone to seal the upset.

R.W. was one of several veterans on that team who provided stability on the field and good character in the locker room. Late in the third quarter, in his role as our punt returner, he'd slipped some guys and broken loose for a twenty-five-yard return, which set up our go-ahead touchdown. You root for a guy like R.W. To see him make that interception, to have that moment in his tenth year in the league and on his fourth team—it was richly deserved.

And so was the fact that we were going to the NFC Championship game.

After the game, in the locker room, I told our guys that I didn't want them talking to the media about the thing with Jerry Jones and the tickets.

—*But Jerry just sent the tickets over, so we're all set*, I said. And the guys erupted.

Tell us we can't do something.

Nobody beats Brett Favre's Packers in Lambeau Field in the playoffs. Too much history. Too much mystique. And it's too cold.

Brandon Jacobs sent the message on our first play from scrimmage when he ran over Charles Woodson. Now everyone knew: We were more than ready for a physical, uncomfortable football game. Our offensive linemen didn't wear sleeves. Eli and Plaxico, two guys from the South, blocked out the minus-twenty-four-degree temperatures and were in perfect sync.

By that point we'd won nine in a row on the road. The "road warriors" thing was a part of our identity.

As for my famous frostbite: I went onto the field for warmups wearing a baseball hat. After about two minutes it felt like my ears were about to fall off. I went back to the locker room and got a winter hat and warmer clothes, but I was still freezing the whole first half. But in the second half, while the cold ate away at my face for all of America to see, I felt nothing. I was completely absorbed in the game, where every play carried the weight of the season.

The lead seesawed back and forth all game. After the Packers tied the game at 20–20 early in the fourth quarter, we had two chances to take the lead: First, with 6:53 remaining, our kicker, Lawrence Tynes, missed a forty-three-yard field goal. Then, as time in regulation expired, with a chance to end the game with a thirty-six-yarder, a bad snap caused Lawrence to miss by a lot. The crowd went wild, ecstatic that their team was still alive. The game went into overtime.

For Lawrence, it had been a trying past few months. Shortly after he came to our team as a free agent, his wife went into premature labor with their twin boys. Lawrence missed minicamp so he could be by her bedside before the boys were born in July. A few months later, during training camp, he was obviously still concerned about their health, and I remember seeing him watching his babies on a webcam. He's a good man and the type of guy you want to have success.

In Green Bay, he'd get another opportunity in overtime. Corey Webster intercepted a Brett Favre pass in Packer territory, giving us possession on their 34. But we only gained five yards on our next three plays, meaning we were set up for a forty-seven-yard field goal—*if* I had faith in Lawrence to make it.

I wasn't sure if I did. He'd said during pregame warmups, when the sun was still out, that 49 yards was the outer limit of his range, but he'd just missed from 43 and 36. Now it was pitch-black outside, much colder than it was during warmups, and Lawrence's foot was black and blue from kicking the rocklike football all game.

I pondered whether or not we should try the field

goal—but then Lawrence made the decision for me. He sprinted out onto the field, and before I knew it, I was watching Lawrence swinging his leg back and forth to warm up.

—*Field goal, field goal!* I yelled.

Some other coaches were skeptical; on my headset, some were talking about the field position we'd give up if Lawrence missed. But I went with my gut.

Tell Lawrence Tynes he can't do something. He knocked it down the pipe. He could've made it from fifty-five yards.

I remember the pandemonium that followed: The raucous locker room. Being given a choice between hot chocolate or soup. Celebrating with my family members and being relieved to hear they'd managed to watch the game *inside* in a box, because I knew they were originally given seats in the stands. Taking forever to peel off my layers upon layers of clothes. Taking that hot shower, knowing we were going to the Super Bowl.

I also remember Col. Greg Gadson. He was on our sideline the whole game. At one point I'd asked him, *You're sure you have enough warm clothes?* and he just looked at me, as if the question was an insult. After Corey Webster made that interception in overtime, the first thing he did was run over to Greg to give him the ball. It's fitting that Greg got that recognition, because that was a game that showed our perseverance and strength in the face of obstacles—values he taught us about several months before.

We were the team of *Tell us we can't do something.* And Greg was the guy who told us that it didn't matter what people said as long as we stuck together and believed in each other.

Chapter Four

A GOOD O-LINE IS LIKE A SYMPHONY

The New York Giants who stepped off the plane in Arizona had gotten in the habit of doing anything and everything needed to get the job done. They had internalized Col. Greg Gadson's message of sacrifice and perseverance to a cause bigger than themselves. Four years later, during our second Super Bowl run, they adopted the mantra *All In* that described this mindset. To be honest, I didn't care for the mantra—shouldn't they have been "All In" the entire time?—but it described the laser focus they had developed, and that no amount of effort would be spared. The same was true of their mindset in 2007.

Case in point: a play Osi Umenyiora made on the Patriots' second series of the game.

To set the scene: Recall that New England had scored a touchdown on their first series. Then, after we'd moved the ball into their territory, they'd intercepted Eli Manning's pass after it bounced off Steve Smith's hands. (The timing of the throw on Steve's in-cut route was slightly off, and the ball got on Steve a little sooner than he'd expected, resulting in an interception by Patriots cornerback Ellis Hobbs. It was Eli's first—and *only*—turnover that postseason. We'd get another chance at Hobbs later in the game.)

Two plays later, the Patriots were at their 42-yard line, facing a third-and-one. This was a critical play. Most people probably don't remember it, but it was one of those hinge plays in a game that are no less important in determining the outcome than the more memorable plays later on. Think of the stakes: If they convert, they're close to midfield, knocking on the door of a field goal that would've increased their lead to seven points, wiping out that first drive we'd felt so good about. Needing just a yard to keep the chains moving, they lined up in a power formation, with two tight ends and an I-formation backfield. Then, they handed the ball to Laurence Maroney for an off-tackle run to their left side—right at Osi.

The Patriots had attacked that side with their running game on their first drive, with success. Teams usually attacked that side on us, choosing to run *away* from Strahan and *at* Osi, whose forte was rushing the quarterback rather than stopping the run. But that didn't mean Osi didn't take a lot of pride in playing the run. After all, he had been mentored by the great Michael Strahan.

At the snap, Patriots tackle Matt Light tried to reach-block Osi to seal him off, so that play could get outside of Osi, and Light got help from a chip from tight end Ben Watson. On a play like this, the expected move for a typical defensive end is to hold his position on the edge to force contain—or, in laypersons' terms, to prevent the ball carrier from getting outside of him.

But Osi wasn't the typical defensive end: Instead of trying to hold his ground, he knifed inside of Light to come directly upfield, essentially gambling on his quickness to cut Maroney off at the pass before he could get outside of him. The gamble paid off; few guys were as quick as Osi, who got a hand on Maroney to trip him up and slow him down, allowing our other defenders to swarm and tackle him for a two-yard loss.

Osi's play was a great example of how a guy who *wants it* badly enough will use the tools at his disposal to get the job done, even if the methods are unconventional. As I always do, I had challenged the guys to play above the X's and O's, because it's those instinctively competitive plays that determine who wins and loses games.

Thanks to Osi's great effort, our defense had forced a three-and-out. It was the defense's first clutch stop on the night. There would be many more.

———

Two plays later came another huge play that showed the competitive grit of our team. The enormity of this play can't be overstated: If David Tyree's "Helmet Catch" is the number one play that helped us win the Super Bowl, this play, with 9:22 to go in the second quarter, was number two.

It was the second play of our third series, a second-and-thirteen: We lined up in the shotgun, and Eli tried to hand the ball off to Ahmad Bradshaw. But they mishandled the exchange, and the ball fell to the ground. Patriots linebacker Pierre Woods appeared to fall onto the ball in the textbook fetal position you coach guys to use. A moment later, Ahmad dived into Woods.

To this day, even after seeing the play multiple times, I still have no idea how Ahmad wrestled that ball free. What I do know is that if he hadn't done that, the Patriots would have had possession at our 30-yard line, already leading 7–3. But somehow Ahmad fought and scrapped and came out of the pile with the ball, and then, for good measure, started jawing in the face of the Patriots Richard

Seymour, who was about nine inches taller and 110 pounds heavier than him. All of it was a testament to Ahmad's feistiness and his competitive will. I've coached many players over many years. None were tougher than Ahmad Bradshaw.

We'd drafted him in the seventh round out of Marshall that off-season, and his role had steadily increased in our last few games. By the playoffs, he was splitting carries about fifty-fifty with Brandon Jacobs, and the two of them were the perfect one-two punch: one huge, one small, both extremely physical.

Ahmad was a forerunner to the types of backs you see in great abundance around the league today: those muscular guys built low to the ground, who don't give defenders a big target to hit. Ahmad got up to top speed very quickly; he could catch the ball and he wasn't afraid of blocking much bigger men. The football adage is that in any physical confrontation, the *low man wins*. Ahmad was confident he always would.

As you can tell, I think the world of the guy, but he wasn't the easiest player to coach and we had some go-arounds. But on Sundays? Ahmad was into the game like few other players I've seen. This kid wanted to win, and he wanted the ball. During games, after offensive series that stalled, he'd come off the field pissed. He wouldn't yell *at* me, but he'd yell loud enough that he was sure I'd hear: *Run the fuckin' ball!*

His emergence late in the season came just at the right time. It was Ahmad who put us into the playoffs with his eighty-eight-yard touchdown run in Buffalo, which sealed the game. That day, there had been snow and sleet and freezing rain, and it was basically assumed that the team going in the direction of the forty-mph wind couldn't score on offense. I can still see Ahmad streaking down the field through the sleet at dusk. It was a literal metaphor for our team at that moment: After a tumultuous last couple of years, the wind was finally at our backs.

Then there was Brandon: It was a stroke of great fortune that Brandon was available when we picked him in the fourth round of the 2005 draft, a raw prospect but one with a rare combination of size and speed. He was six foot three, 265 pounds—and *fast*. If there was a crack for him to get started, look out. Defensive backs would always underestimate his speed and take the wrong angle in the open field, unable to comprehend that such a big man could be so fast.

His bread and butter, of course, was his punishing style. *Punishing.* Teams didn't want any part of tackling him, and the unpleasant task of being forced to do so all game had an impact beyond the box score. The signature carry of his career was the opening play against Green Bay in the NFC Championship game, when he ran over Hall of Famer Charles Woodson, which was just a colossal hit. Sometimes, a hit in a football game can change everything about it, and every*thing* and every-*one* participating in the game isn't the same after that. Brandon's hit on Woodson was one of those moments. I can still *hear* it.

Which is fitting, because you could always hear Brandon. He was talkative and bubbly, with a big, loud laugh. Big in stature, big in personality. A caring, loyal man. How can you not love a guy like that?

One time after he'd retired, he came by the facility to check out a practice; I was happy to see him because he's a great guy—he's one of many ex-players who have helped out with the Jay Fund—and he always brought a positive energy. But the *volume*—at a certain point I had to tell him, *Brandon, would you mind? We're conducting a practice here.*

He laughed and took it well. That's the way he was about everything.

One last thing about Brandon that I'll always appreciate: He loved being an NFL player and was very proud to be a New York Giant. And he'd be the first to tell you that.

I'm sure that a big reason why Brandon loved being a Giant is the offensive line he ran behind.

I always tell people that you can close your eyes during a practice and be able to tell if an offensive line is good or not. You can *hear* the power surge off the ball, the togetherness, even the breathing. I remember watching a training tape of Bo Schembechler's Michigan team, from ages ago, when Hall of Famer Dan Dierdorf played there, and I could hear the synchronized execution of these huge, great athletes. *That* sound—it's music to the ears of anyone who truly loves the sport. It's what all coaches are striving for. And in that era, with the Giants, our offensive line sounded like a symphony.

David Diehl, Rich Seubert, Shaun O'Hara, Chris Snee, and Kareem McKenzie. They came to us from different places—two of them were former undrafted free agents—and were molded into the best offensive line in Giants history by position coach Pat Flaherty. By the 2007 Super Bowl, they'd been playing together for several years. The following year, 2008, they dominated the league, and articles were being written saying they should collectively win the NFL's MVP.

Diehl was a guard by trade who'd moved to left tackle before the '07 season. It showed how team oriented David was, but it worried many observers because David didn't look the part of the prototypical long-limbed left tackle. What those observers didn't realize was that *mentally*, David was perfectly suited for the position. If you're a left tackle, no matter how good you are, you're going to be matched up against the other team's best pass rusher, and that guy's gonna make some plays. The key is bouncing back on the next play, so that a bad play doesn't lead to a bad series or a bad game—and that was where David set himself apart. His confidence was bullet-proof. He never got down on himself, and he never doubted that he'd beat the man across from him on the next play.

Another thing about having David over there was that it gave us an advantage in the running game. Most teams are very right-side run heavy, because the left tackle is built for pass blocking and usually isn't as physical in the running game. But David was great in the running game, and while we still favored the right side on running plays, we were able to keep teams honest, because our left side was really strong as well. It was an advantage that was subtle, but the production of our running game spoke for itself.

To David's right, Richie Seubert, our left guard, was the toughest guy I've ever been around. In 2003, he suffered a gruesome spiral fracture in his right leg that kept him out for two years, put him in the hospital for five months, and required multiple surgeries—including a skin graft up his leg that's about two inches wide. He'd been on IR for a long time when I got to the Giants, and I wondered why we were keeping him around. The answer became obvious when I saw him working harder than I've ever seen anyone work to get back onto the field. And when he returned, he was, miraculously, every bit the excellent player and emotional leader he'd been two years before. He was unconquerable.

And feisty. His first year fully back from his injury, I swear he got into a fight every single day of training camp. But what made Richie great was that he was the perfect combination of on the edge but also coachable. On power running plays to our right side, Richie would be the pulling guard, which required quick calculations about which guy to block—cleaning up a guy at the line of scrimmage, a linebacker, a safety sometimes—and how to block them to clear a path for the runner. A hunting and fishing kid from Wisconsin who'd been an undrafted free agent, Richie might have downplayed his intellect, but the guy was really smart and always made the right decisions on the field. That skin graft on his right leg might as well have been another metaphor for our team: We'd been through a lot and it sometimes looked ugly, but we kept fighting, no matter what.

Our center, Shaun O'Hara, was exactly what he's

like on television as an NFL Network analyst: Mr. Personality, well-groomed, extremely smart. He's a guy who cares deeply about people—he was the players union rep and he runs a charity, the Shaun O'Hara Foundation, that battles rare diseases that don't get a lot of funding. But in the locker room, he joined Richie as the biggest ball-busters on the team—those guys could've taken their act on the road.

Shaun had been an undrafted free agent like Richie, and he wasn't the biggest guy—he played at 290 pounds—but he was quick and crafty. He excelled as a combination blocker: As the center, he'd often have to snap the ball and get his head across a nose tackle who was shaded to his front shoulder, before continuing to a linebacker on the second level. Shaun was quick and athletic enough to do all of that.

At right tackle was Kareem McKenzie, a battleship-sized man who was the perfect anchor for our running game. Before the 2005 season, Dave Gettleman and the rest of our pro personnel staff were doing cartwheels when he became available as a free agent, and he was one of several key signings we made before that season along with Plaxico Burress and Antonio Pierce. He was quiet, proud, and extremely smart—he'd always have a book in his bag, and now he works as a counselor for disadvantaged young people while pursuing his PhD. Kareem was a very pleasant guy and everyone loved him, but he wasn't a talker. Whenever O'Hara, Seubert, and Diehl started up with their usual shenanigans, Kareem would just smile and give them an eyebrow. He was the adult in the room.

Then there was Chris Snee, our right guard and my son-in-law, and the best player on that outstanding offensive line. Let me be clear for the record: Chris Snee should be in the Hall of Fame. He was that good, year in and year out, until an elbow injury cut short his ten-year career in 2013.

His strong suit was *power*, which he built up in the weight room, where he was more dedicated than any player I ever coached. He'd go up against 320-pound defensive tackles and he'd overpower them consistently, using his strength, plus his footwork and leverage, to put himself in good positions. Chris and Linval Joseph, a defensive tackle we drafted in 2011 who has had an excellent NFL career, were the strongest Giants during my time there, and Chris combined that raw strength with athleticism—he'd been a good high school basketball player with a lot of spring in his legs, and even today, at forty, he can dunk.

Every week, as a coaching staff, we'd look at the personnel matchups and label them a plus or a minus, depending on which player had the advantage. Chris was as durable as he was dominant: For more than nine years, for all of those games, we labeled him a plus every single week except for one game he missed in 2011. It was a great way to start a game plan.

As for his personality, Chris is an ornery guy with a heart of gold. He'd come to work with a chip on his shoulder and he'd bring that nasty edge to the field. He's extremely smart too—he was selected for the National Honor Society in high school—but most days, you couldn't get anything but grunts and one-word answers from him. But that's just one side of a man I'm honored to call my family member. He's got a mean streak when it comes to football, but he's a kind, devoted husband and father. When it comes to their four kids, Chris and my daughter Kate have an equal partnership. Changing diapers when the kids were babies, preparing meals, or driving them hours to games—whatever it is, Chris is an A+ father just as he was a player.

He'll do anything for the Jay Fund as well. Every Christmas, Chris and Kate visit the pediatric cancer ward at St. Joseph's University Medical Center in Paterson and give out presents they've personally bought and wrapped. He brings my grandkids, teaching them the important lesson that not every child is so fortunate.

When we drafted Chris, the family connection wasn't a factor at all; he was simply the best player on our board. We had a mid-first-round grade on him, and when he fell to us in the second round, people in our draft room were high-fiving each other. I'd first seen him in 2002, before the draft, when I was still with the Jaguars, and I went up to Boston College to look at their game film to study a running back, William Green, who wound up being drafted in the first round. But the guy who jumped out at me was a guard who had every defender on skates. I kept asking, *Who's 76?*

At the time, my daughter Kate was also a student at BC. Before Kate and I went out for dinner that night, she asked if she could bring a friend. I don't think Chris said a word the entire dinner—he just sat there, eating.

When we both got to the Giants in 2004, mixing family with business was never uncomfortable because of the type of guy Chris was. You couldn't see how hard Chris worked, how quickly he grasped concepts, how accountable he was, and think that I was giving him any special treatment. I've often said that I don't fine players, players fine themselves— and something that speaks volumes about Chris is that he was *never* fined, which is unique among the players who played for me for multiple years. That wasn't because he got special treatment. It was because he was never late for anything and never broke any rules.

So that was our offensive line, the backbone of our offense. Our bread-and-butter running plays were 36/37 power (your basic off-tackle play) as well as a sprint draw to the open side or a toss sweep to the strong side. We ran these plays often and we ran them well. We didn't let complexity get in the way of execution.

Between our offensive line and our defensive line, it's a toss-up of which unit was the strength of our team in those days, but there's no doubt that those two units going against each other in training camp and practice brought out the best in everybody. And when your line play is that good, on both sides of the ball, you have a chance against anybody.

Even the 18-0 New England Patriots.

And on our fourth drive of the game, which began with 6:45 to go in the second quarter at our own 43-yard line, our running game finally clicked into place. We needed that to happen: Going into that series, our previous four offensive plays had been the interception off Steve's fingertips, a sack, the muffed exchange between Eli and Ahmad, and an incomplete pass. So we decided to run the ball.

On our second play of the series, we popped a thirteen-yard run to Ahmad. It was an inside zone run play, but Ahmad read it well and bounced it *outside*, then got upfield in a hurry. He could have taken it for major yardage had not Patriots safety James Sanders gotten a hand on his foot to slow him down a bit before Rodney Harrison tackled him. After the play, Ahmad stood up and gestured with his hand that he was *this close* to breaking a big one.

On the next play, our line got a decent push off the right side and Brandon followed them, grinding ahead for four yards. On the play after that, Brandon ran right, following a pulling Snee and slamming ahead for seven yards, finishing the play by running over Patriots linebacker Tedy Bruschi, one of the best run-stuffing linebackers of the era.

That gave us a first-and-ten at the Patriots' 31-yard line, in field goal range. The sequence let the Patriots know that nearly one half into the game, we wouldn't back down from our physical game plan. It also showed we could run to our right in addition to our left. At that point, after Brandon's run, we had been *perfectly* balanced in terms of run versus pass, having run fourteen running plays and fourteen passing plays.

After twenty-six minutes, some things had gone our way and some things hadn't. But we liked where we stood. This was our kind of game.

———

Unfortunately, our drive stalled after that. We picked up six yards on the next two plays, setting up a manageable third-and-four. But then Adalius Thomas, the Patriots' veteran edge rusher, made a big play for them—the type of play that *our* pass rushers were making all night for us.

A quick digression: The stadium we were playing in, University of Phoenix Stadium, presented almost no adverse conditions. It was climate controlled, with a good playing surface, and there was nothing about the setting that benefited either team.

But it was indoors, and when you're playing indoors, everything is loud and it feels like the crowd is right on top of you. On a big third-down play, with the fans excited, being indoors meant we had to use a silent snap count. A little later in the game, this would become an advantage for us, when Michael Strahan jumped the Patriots' silent count on third down for a key sack of Brady. But this time, Thomas, who gave us fits all game, jumped our count and got the edge against David Diehl on Eli's blind side. Thomas flushed Eli out of the pocket, ran him down, and tomahawked the ball out of Eli's right hand.

Once again, Ahmad was the only person on our offense near the fumble, and Ahmad, ever scrappy, beat Mike Vrabel to the ball. But instead of trying to recover it, he swatted it forward about ten yards downfield, where Steve Smith recovered it on the sideline. The play showed Ahmad's instinctive competitiveness: In his mind, by batting the ball forward, I'm sure he was trying to advance it forward to get us close to a first down. Unfortunately, batting the ball forward is against the rules, and we were penalized ten yards from the spot of the foul, pushing us back to our 39, out of field goal range, for a third-and-eighteen.

We were extremely lucky that Steve fell on the ball: Like Ahmad, Steve was a rookie whose presence and sense of the moment was beyond his years—something we saw plenty of times that night.

We were also fortunate on the next play, on third down, when Patriots defensive back Randall Gay *just* missed a diving interception attempt on a ball thrown into triple coverage. This brought up fourth down, with no choice but to punt, and Jeff Feagles's punt pushed the Patriots back to their 11. They took over with 1:47 to go.

It was frustrating: On three of our first four drives, we'd had first downs at the Patriots' 17-, 19-, and 31-yard lines. But with those three great opportunities, we'd come away with just three points.

Now we were in a position we didn't want to be in: The Patriots had the ball in the two-minute drill to end the first half, and then they'd get the ball to start the second half. We were down by four points, and the greatest offense in league history had two chances to extend the lead.

We needed our defense to step up. We were confident they would.

Chapter Five

———

YOU HAVE TO KNOCK TOM BRADY DOWN

Let's go back to the Patriots' first play from scrimmage that night. It said a lot about what was going to happen for the rest of the game.

Tom Brady took the snap from under center. He faked a handoff to running back Laurence Maroney, and a moment later, he faked another handoff to Wes Welker on an end around. All of that was misdirection to set up a screen pass: Maroney, the intended receiver, leaked into the flat, where three Patriots linemen were ready to block for him once he caught the ball. But he never did; Brady's pass fell a few yards short of him.

The reason? Our nose tackle, Barry Cofield, didn't chase the misdirection. He charged right at

Brady and got in his face as he threw, knocking him to the ground, hard.

Yes, the Patriots scored a touchdown on that drive. But that play was significant because it sent two messages: One, that we weren't overanxious and susceptible to the misdirection; however explosive the Patriots were, regardless of what they'd done to us in our previous meeting in Week 17, we were going to maintain our discipline on defense. And two, we were going to knock Tom Brady on his ass. He'd been too comfortable in the previous game. This one would be different.

Hitting Tom Brady was the only way we'd have a chance to slow down that offense. We knew they were the greatest scoring machine in NFL history, just like we knew Brady was the best quarterback to ever play the game. But we also knew he was human, and that there's not a quarterback alive whose performance doesn't suffer when he's hit hard and hit often.

Brady's as tough as they come, but if you knock any quarterback down repeatedly, he starts to wear down and *expect* it, and when a quarterback is looking for where the next hit is coming from, that throws off everything. While the Patriots were putting up all those points in 2007, Brady had mostly been kept off the ground: He'd been sacked on just

3.5 percent of his dropbacks, fifth best in the league among full-time starters. That was a credit both to the Patriots' offensive line and to Brady's intelligence. The Super Bowl had to be different. Otherwise, we stood no chance.

The first play was a sign of things to come. We knocked him down on that play and then knocked him down sixteen more times, including five sacks. The execution of our schemes, the winning of individual matchups by our players—it never stopped. All these years later, the accomplishment has only grown in my eyes. If anything, in my opinion, it's overlooked by people who talk and write about these things. But here's what I think: Considering the stakes, considering the opponent, what our defense did that night was the greatest defensive performance in the history of the sport.

———

The pressure on Brady is why we won that game. And pressure packages were what I was looking for when I brought in Steve Spagnuolo, then the Eagles' linebackers coach, to interview for our open defensive coordinator position in January 2007.

During his interview, Steve stayed at our facility for ten hours. Time flies when you're having fun. His positive energy was obvious from the get-go. So was his knowledge of ways to get after the quarterback. He was a protégé of Jim Johnson, the longtime Eagles defensive coordinator known as a master architect of blitz packages, and I thought our defense needed that aggressive philosophy. Steve saw a roster that included names like Michael Strahan, Osi Umenyiora, Justin Tuck, and Mathias Kiwanuka and saw the materials *he* needed to put his ideas into action.

I was impressed with everything about Steve. He was forty-seven years old and in great physical shape, upbeat and sharp. We talked about his upbringing in Grafton, Massachusetts, not far from where I'd coached at BC. We talked about our shared connection, Jack Bicknell, the former BC head coach who'd hired me to be quarterbacks coach in 1981 (where I coached Doug Flutie), then hired Steve to his staff when he went to NFL Europe. By the end of the day I was convinced this was a man ready for his moment—a man who'd bring exactly what we needed.

More than anything, our defense needed an identity. In previous years, our defensive strategy would change week to week based on the opponent. We had talented players, but I felt we hadn't reached our ceiling on that side of the ball. We were the New York Giants, after all, a franchise with a proud tradition of defense, and I thought Steve's attacking style would inspire our players to make their own contribution to that tradition. Defensive players have more fun when they're being proactive rather than reactive; if you're coaching an attacking style, you're gonna get better buy-in from your players.

And that was exactly what happened; the guys took to him immediately. Steve is what I call a force multiplier, with a personality and positive approach that boosts everyone around him. On the chalkboard in his defensive meeting room, he'd write a biblical saying from Proverbs 27:17 that described what he was trying to instill: "As iron sharpens iron, so one man sharpens another."

Like me, Steve was a grinder. For him, as with me, five hours of sleep was a luxurious night. At 5:15 in the morning, we'd bump into each other in the weight room, and it was an unspoken race for who could get there first to control the music. If Steve beat me, he'd play rock. If I beat him, I'd play Sinatra ("New York, New York" always got me going).

He was the right man for the job and I knew it—even when the defense got off to an awful start. After two games, we were 0-2. And our defense had given up eighty points.

I don't read the papers, but I can only imagine what they were saying. The media wanted me out of town after the previous season, and here we were, behind the eight ball, with the new defensive coordinator I'd just hired overseeing a unit that had given up the most points in the league.

They say you only really learn about someone by how they react to adversity, and I learned a lot about Steve after that. His positivity and his belief in himself and our players never wavered. If you've given up eighty points, it means players have made mistakes, and those mistakes need to be pointed out and corrected. But Steve, knowing his players were grasping a new system, made the corrections without deflating their spirits. Everything with him was a positive learning experience, and the players came away believing that if they did things as he coached them, they'd be successful.

And then what happened? The goal-line stop against Washington in Week 3, which turned the season around. The backstory of the fourth-down stop speaks volumes. Before that decisive play, Washington indicated they would line up without a huddle, and I asked Steve if he wanted to take a time-out to get our players organized; if I had to decide on my own, I probably would have. But Steve said no—he had faith in his guys to step up, and he called the same defense as the play before. I trusted Steve, just like Steve trusted his players. We stopped them, won the game, and our defense really never looked back. We rattled off six wins in a row—never giving up more than 284 yards in a game during that stretch.

Every Friday that season, Steve and I would sit down to review our blitz packages. He'd go over the blitzes he'd put in and tell me why he thought they would be effective. I remember how excited he'd get when talking about the schemes. This guy was *passionate* about getting after the quarterback. You could see it in his eyes.

Rushing the passer was a focus of our organization at the time, and in that regard we were ahead of the curve. In 2007, under Steve, we implemented what became known as our NASCAR package, when we'd bring in four defensive ends on third downs to pressure the quarterback. It was a natural response to the talent we had on our team and an acknowledgment of what the league had become— one in which quarterbacks had become super performers, and the only chance defenses had to slow them down was to put pressure on them.

The year before, we'd used our first-round pick on Mathias Kiwanuka, a talented defensive end from Boston College, despite having a surplus of talent at the position. Late in the '07 season, we gave Tuck a sizable contract extension, despite the fact that he was technically not a starter. All of it was an acknowledgment of a phrase you often heard when it came to the Giants in that era: You can never have too many pass rushers.

Our pass rush carried our defense that year. Our fifty-two sacks led the league, part of a unit that gave up the seventh fewest total yards and the fifth fewest yards per drive. We'd given up thirty-eight points to the Patriots in Week 17, but by then, we were used to facing adversity without getting discouraged. To Steve Spagnuolo and his defense, giving up all those points in Week 17 wasn't a sign of more bad things to come. It was an opportunity to make corrections.

He went back to the lab. He devised ways to bring pressure. We benefited from the fact that Corey Webster, our third-year cornerback, had made a tremendous leap the previous three games and was playing with great confidence by the time we got to the Super Bowl. Teamed with Aaron Ross, our rookie corner who was having an excellent first year, we felt confident in our defensive backs to hold up, which would enable us to take some more risks in getting to the passer.

Which is what we needed to do. That much was obvious after the Week 17 game, when Steve came up to me to assess what went wrong.

—*We just didn't get to him enough,* he said.

———

On the Patriots' third series, we absolutely needed to get to Brady. They'd scored on their first drive and we'd stopped them three and out on their next series. But after we went three and out ourselves, they took over on their 30-yard line with 8:35 remaining in the half. They would also get the ball to start the second half, so a stop here was imperative. You don't want to be behind multiple scores to the 2007 Patriots.

We stopped a Maroney run for no gain on their first-down play. On second down, Steve decided to dial something up. It was a blitz involving our middle linebackers, Antonio Pierce and Kawika Mitchell, as well as our nickel corner in the slot, Aaron Ross. The design of the blitz was brilliant—and the execution was perfect.

Here's how it went: Before the snap, both Antonio and Kawika threatened to blitz inside, on opposite sides of the center, with Antonio a few feet to the left of the center and Kawika a shade to the right of the center (from the perspective of the defense). But at the snap, both turned their bodies away from the line of scrimmage, as if they were dropping into pass coverage.

Just as they did so, Aaron, who was lined up in the slot on the defensive left side, came on a blitz. His blitz drew center Dan Koppen's attention; Koppen, convinced that neither Antonio nor Kawika would blitz, shuffled to his right to help with Aaron's rush. Running back Kevin Faulk, whose job on the play was blitz pickup, also saw Aaron coming and went to block him.

But Kawika had fooled them: After taking his first step back, he stuck his foot in the ground and charged forward toward Brady. The center, Koppen, didn't see him coming, and Kawika came untouched for the sack. It was the type of thing any football coach dreams about when they're drawing something up on the board, and it put the Patriots in a third-and-seventeen.

Here's the thing about that game: The scheme, the defenders' ability to win individual matchups, and the down-and-distance situation all combined to produce the best possible outcome for our pass rush. Case in point was the following play, the first of Justin Tuck's two sacks on the night.

Justin was the breakout star of that game, but in our building, we already knew how good he was, and we had a good feeling about lining him up inside against a guard. The Patriots' left guard, Logan Mankins, was an outstanding football player— he made seven Pro Bowls in his career—but asking any guard to pass block twenty-four-year-old Justin Tuck just isn't fair. Especially when the pass protectors have so many other things to worry about, like

Steve's blitzes, as well as two guys named Umeny-iora and Strahan. And now it's third-and-seventeen, and Justin doesn't have to worry about stopping the run and can focus on pinning his ears back and getting after Brady.

That was exactly what he did on the play: He fired off the ball way too quickly for Mankins, beating him to the outside. Mankins scrambled to get his feet in position to catch up, but it was hopeless. Justin sacked Brady from the blind side.

When he did, the crowd reacted. That low, passionate, only-in-New-York roar. It was another moment that made us realize this was a Giants crowd. Our fans gained confidence, our team gained confidence. Maybe most of America expected the Patriots to go up and down the field on us and score something close to the thirty-eight points they'd scored in Week 17. But we didn't.

After the sack, Brady stayed down on the grass for a few moments. He wasn't hurt, he was frustrated. He'd had about enough of getting hit. After two straight three and outs, his night wasn't going according to plan.

———

But for our defense, this was exactly the kind of game we had envisioned.

After our ensuing drive stalled, the Patriots got the ball back at their 11-yard line, with 1:47 remaining in the half. Once again, our defense faced a tall task: stopping Brady in a two-minute drill and then turning around and stalling that offense after halftime. Fail to do either of those things and we would have faced a two-score deficit. During the '07 season, the Patriots had scored ninety points in the last two minutes of halves—by far the most in the NFL.

On the Patriots' first play, they lined up in a shotgun formation. Even though it was first down, the two-minute drill dictated that it was a passing situation, so in response, Steve dialed up another masterpiece of a blitz.

Before the snap, Antonio threatened to blitz by creeping up to the line of scrimmage just to the right of the center from the defense's perspective— the same spot Kawika had rushed from on his sack the previous series. From the slot on that same side, Aaron Ross also threatened the line of scrimmage. I don't know this for sure, but watching the game all these years later, it looks like Brady noticed the threat of the blitz from his left and changed the protection in response.

But at the snap, both Antonio and Aaron sprinted back into coverage. Instead, we brought two guys from the *other* side, the defensive left side. This beat the offensive protection, which slid away to the other side—probably in response to what Antonio and Aaron were doing before the snap.

The blitzers coming from the defensive left side were slot nickelback Kevin Dockery and safety Gibril Wilson. Dockery came inside, and he was picked up by running back Kevin Faulk. This meant that there was nobody to pick up Wilson, who crashed in from the outside and knocked Brady down as he threw, forcing a wobbly throw that fell well short of Randy Moss, who was streaking down the field on the left side.

A note on Gibril Wilson, who was an outstanding blitzer from the safety position for years: Super Bowl XLII was the last game he'd play for us; that off-season, we lost him as a free agent to the Raiders. Gibril loved to have his number dialed on blitzes. What made him good at it was his sense of timing, his understanding of the overall scheme and the angles he'd have to take, as well as his short burst of speed to close on the quarterback. On this play, because of the design of the blitz, he didn't have to beat anybody, but it's still a credit to him that he got to Brady in time to disrupt the pass. It might have looked easy and straightforward, but not every safety would have gotten there—and it was one of many examples in that game in which the scheme and the players' execution worked hand in hand.

Another notable aspect of that play is that it

showed how we were able to limit Randy Moss, who had a touchdown later in the game but caught only 5 balls on 12 targets for 62 yards—far below his season average of about 93 yards, with a 61 percent catch rate. He's an all-time great with deep speed that's unmatched in the history of the sport. He showcased this speed in our Week 17 meeting when he caught a bomb for a sixty-five-yard touchdown, blowing past our Cover 2 for a game-sealing touchdown. In that game, he torched us for 100 yards and two touchdowns, so we needed an answer for him.

We double-covered him for most of the game, usually with a corner playing to the outside of him and a safety inside—but you can't double-cover a guy on *every* play and basically announce to the opposition that you'll only be using nine defenders on the rest of their offense. Given that, the key element to stopping Moss was getting to the quarterback. Because to get a guy like him downfield, a quarterback needs time. And we didn't give their quarterback any.

This was on display again several plays later—after the Patriots had converted a third-and-thirteen to get out to their 26—and they decided to take a deep shot to Moss on the offensive right side. On the play, Moss, running a go route, got behind cornerback Corey Webster and safety James Butler, with nobody between him and the end zone: From that aspect, it looked exactly like his touchdown in Week 17.

But Osi and Tuck, both rushing from the defensive right side, got home *just* quickly enough to rush Brady by a fraction of a tick, which prevented him from executing the proper mechanics on his throw. Brady's pass sailed over Moss's head as Osi and Tuck converged on him and brought him to the ground. Had they gotten there any later, it's possible that play would have gone for a seventy-four-yard touchdown. But it didn't—an example of how the little things in a football game are inseparable from the big things.

————

Osi and Tuck weren't done on that drive. The Patriots wound up finally completing a pass to Moss, an eighteen-yarder, his first catch of the game, after which he went out of bounds with twenty-two seconds left in the half. This gave them a first-and-ten at our 44-yard line. They had no time-outs but had some time to work with; at that point, the odds were pretty good that they'd manage enough yardage to attempt a field goal. Brady, frustrated for most of the night, now had a spring in his step and a familiar determined look on his face as he got his guys positioned. At that moment, the Patriots had momentum and we were on our heels. We needed a play.

Brady took the snap and looked downfield. Moss made a move at the line and streaked down the offensive right side. Brady geared up to take a shot downfield. We rushed just our front four. The fate of the play likely rested on whether or not our defensive linemen could beat the blockers in front of them.

Lucky for us, Justin Tuck was on our team. Once again rushing from the defensive tackle spot against Mankins, Justin beat him to the outside and then made a hard left turn to chase Brady, who had slid to his right and stepped up in the pocket to buy himself more time. Brady patted the ball in preparation to throw a bomb that could potentially give his team control of the game. He cocked his arm back, and was milliseconds away from heaving it downfield when Justin swatted it from his grip with his big right hand, crashing into his blind side a moment later.

The ball came loose, and Osi, who had worked toward Brady with an inside spin move and hit him as well, recovered it for us. On the ground, he was swarmed by Patriots trying to rip the ball away from him. But Osi wasn't giving that thing up.

It was a beautiful play for a football coach to watch, a classic for the teaching reel. Justin flattened out his rush at *just* the right moment, and went for the ball just like he's supposed to. And it was no surprise that Osi, who was blessed with terrific hand-eye coordination and displayed his nose for the football time and again for us during his career, was the guy to recover it.

That's how the first half of Super Bowl XLII ended, with Tom Brady on the ground after a strip sack. He's a great, great competitor—we knew we hadn't heard the last from him. But we also knew that during Brady's historic season, he'd been accustomed to having a certain amount of time, and he wasn't getting that tonight.

———

When it comes to media coverage of the NFL, you hear a lot about "halftime adjustments." But the idea that coaches go in at halftime and make radical game plan adjustments is misleading. The fact is, we're making adjustments after every single play.

During halftime of Super Bowl XLII, trailing 7–3, we made no major adjustments. There were no big rah-rah speeches or emotional moments. We were confident, believing we had no reason to deviate from what we'd been doing. On offense, despite scoring only three points, we'd actually moved the ball pretty well. On our four drives, we totaled 121 yards, about 30 yards per drive, which was more than the 28 yards per drive we'd averaged during the season.

The picture was even better on defense, where we'd given up just 87 yards. To put that in perspective, we were on pace to give up 174 yards, compared to the 419 yards the Patriots averaged in 2007. And our strong defensive play continued on the Patriots' first drive of the second half. They picked up two first downs but then stalled, and faced a fourth-and-two at our 44-yard line.

It was a kind of no-man's-land, where it wasn't clear whether the Patriots would go for it or punt. Amid this uncertainty, Bill Belichick pulled something from up his sleeve.

Here's what happened: We were in what we called our "defensive stay," which is when you have your defense on the field, except the punt returner is swapped in for the deep safety. This hedges against the possibility that the Patriots will go for it or fake a punt, but having the punt returner back deep allows you to make a fair catch if they do indeed punt. Belichick kept his offense on the field for a bit—but then he rushed his punt team out.

In response, we swapped our regular punt return

team in for our "defensive stay," but in all the confusion, we had twelve men on the field when the Patriots snapped the ball. The five-yard penalty gave the Patriots a first down. The officials actually missed this in real time, but Belichick, who knew he'd caught us, challenged the play, and the replay showed our player trying to sprint off the field but failing to do so by half a stride.

On the sideline, I was completely beside myself about what had happened. The Patriots had done this before; it was something we'd prepared for. Later, the NFL would actually change the rule, mandating that if the offensive team substitutes in this situation, the umpire has to stand over the ball and allow the defensive team the time to substitute as well. But during this game, this loophole existed—and the Patriots exploited it to their advantage, undoing a critical defensive stop and dealing us a major psychological blow. It honestly still makes me mad: To think that this play could have cost us a Super Bowl...it would have been a tragedy.

So there I was, in a slow burn, pacing the sideline looking for an official whose rear end I could tear apart. The red line in my face was rising—until Michael Strahan slid up next to me.

—*Coach*, he said. *We've been in much tougher situations than this.*

He was completely calm, looking straight ahead

at the field as he addressed me. Those few words told me a lot. They told me Michael would make sure that the defense would go back and do the job regardless of the circumstances. They told me he'd personally see to it that his teammates reacted the right way.

They did. After the Patriots picked up a first down on their next set—on third-and-thirteen, a checkdown to Kevin Faulk that went for fourteen, another punch to the stomach—our defense stepped up, limiting the Patriots to three yards in the next two plays to set up a third-and-seven.

That was when Michael, who was a great student of the game, put his impressive football IQ to use. With the play clock winding down, Brady, who was lined up in the shotgun, picked his knee up as a signal to his offense. But Michael had a feel for the silent shotgun snap count. He knew that because there were only two seconds remaining on the play clock, the ball would be snapped the moment Brady's foot came down. And when Brady's foot hit the ground, Michael fired out of his stance a quarter beat *before* the ball was snapped.

It was a calculated risk that paid off, because Michael wasn't offsides and Patriots right tackle Stephen Neal didn't stand a chance. Michael flew past him on the outside and then sacked Brady for a six-yard loss. Of all the great plays Michael Strahan made in his Hall of Fame career for the Giants, that was the most important.

Faced with a fourth-and-thirteen on their next play, from our 31, Belichick opted against trying a forty-nine-yard field goal. (Would Stephen Gostkowski have made that field goal? Would history had been different if he tried? We'll never know.) Instead, the Patriots tried a passing play. We rushed only four guys to focus on our downfield coverage, but Osi eventually beat two blockers to get home, forcing Brady to throw the ball away, out of the end zone.

That was four straight drives without points for the Patriots. Just as Michael had assured me, he and the defense were up to the task of weathering another tough situation.

That whole sequence—Michael's statement to me on the sideline, and then his clutch sack—was an illustration of something I always say when people ask me about Michael: that he's the greatest natural leader I've ever been around.

———

With Michael, it all started with his incredible capacity for work. You've seen this in his postfootball life: His comfort and ease on TV may seem natural, as if things come easily to him, but it's the product of a lot of hard work. I remember once trying to get ahold of him on a Saturday for something related to the Jay Fund, my charity, and he was filming an episode of *The $100,000 Pyramid*. It blew my mind to think about: The guy's up in the predawn hours every day for his morning show on ABC, and then he spends his Saturdays filming *another* show. The guy is absolutely tireless, just like he was when I coached him, the type of person who constantly embraces challenges and then works and works and works until he conquers them.

The same was true of his football career. As a child he was overweight, but his father, a military man, put him on a workout program to get him into shape. Maybe it was because he had to face challenges so early in life that he wasn't afraid of them.

Before his senior year of high school, he went to live with his uncle in football-crazy Houston, and even though he'd never played against good competition before, he worked his way into being recruited by Texas Southern University. He was a star there and was drafted early in the second round by the Giants, but it wasn't an easy path: He missed half his rookie year with a foot injury, and being drafted as a relative unknown from a small program meant he had a lot to prove. Add in the fact that he broke into the league as the low man on the totem pole on a defense that included Lawrence Taylor, spending his rookie year fetching LT's dry cleaning. The point is that Michael learned early on that anything he accomplished in this league, he'd have to earn.

And he accomplished a lot. He made seven Pro Bowls, he won the Defensive Player of the Year Award and he set the single-season sack record—an especially remarkable feat considering Michael was a left defensive end, working on the power side, where his primary responsibility was stopping the run, which he did exceptionally well. In that spot, he'd always have tight ends chipping down on him, and he didn't have the advantage of coming from the quarterback's blind side.

As a pass rusher, Michael had a lot of good attributes, but the most important of all was that he was smart. He studied the opponent and knew the strengths and weaknesses of the guy he was going against, and over the years his tremendous knowledge only increased. He was a great athlete who played with very good balance and leverage, and technically, he was completely sound in his footwork and his hands. He was relentless—the guy just didn't get tired as the game wore on. Nobody on the field was better conditioned than him, and he used that to his advantage.

As the years went on, he knew that to compensate for aging, and the impact getting older has on quickness, he needed to lose weight. He was listed at 275 pounds when he broke the sack record in 2001, but I'd estimate that by '07 he was playing at about 240 pounds, squaring up against right tackles all in excess of 300 pounds. By that point, his knowledge, technique, and anticipation were so good that his strength didn't suffer at all. He played much bigger than he was, which showed how well he knew his body and how he had to train to be at his best. It also showed his extraordinary discipline.

So did the way he practiced. He'd been very close with his first defensive line coach, Earl Leggett, who taught him how to practice, which Michael never forgot. He'd run to the ball, play after play, with more tenacity than any player I've ever coached. It didn't matter where he was or where the ballcarrier was—he could be the defensive end on the other side of a sweep, with the runner headed to the far sideline—and Michael would sprint and touch the ballcarrier. You have to understand the example it sets when your best defensive player is also your hardest worker. If the Hall of Famer is going full-bore, all the time, the rest of the guys are gonna see that and be inspired by what's possible with that kind of effort. If Michael Strahan, owner of the single-season sack record, is giving 100 percent in practice, how can the other guys not?

Michael inspired with his work ethic. He also inspired with his charisma. Now that millions of Americans watch him every morning, it's not news to anyone that Michael is an extremely personable, upbeat guy who's fun to be around. I remember watching some footage of him walking through the streets of Manhattan, and every person on the street, every doorman, every cab driver, was his best friend. That was the energy he brought to the locker room.

He was able to convey his passion for the game and our team very spontaneously. The 2007 season was when Michael started his "Stomp you out" chant before games. He'd be charged through with emotion; one day, jumping high in the air and coming down just came to him, and it became a rallying cry. Some guys went along with it, other guys thought it was corny, but Michael didn't care. He was gonna express his enthusiasm, and he had the force of personality where that enthusiasm spilled over to his teammates. Michael kept doing his "Stomp you out" thing before games week after week. Eventually, we kept winning week after week.

———

Michael and I have high regard for each other, but it took us a while to get to that point. Things between us got off on the wrong foot. When we first met, Michael had already decided he didn't like me. He was the leader of a team that had fallen on hard times. I was the coach brought in to instill a sense of discipline and pride, and my reputation as a disciplinarian unafraid to break a few eggs to make an omelet preceded me.

I'd been brought up in the game learning there was a right way to do things, and I had rules to that effect—about how players should wear their socks to prevent injuries, about how we should sit in meetings, and of course the well-known one that we should show up to meetings five minutes before the appointed time. Michael had heard the caricature version of me filtered through the media and had made up his mind: He'd play one year for me, then go somewhere else.

He has said as much. In the NFL Network's *A Football Life* documentary episode about me, Michael says, *When I first met Coach Coughlin, it wasn't a "dislike." It was a hate. Hated him.*

The first time Michael came into my office, he had an expression on his face that made it obvious we weren't gonna be having coffee and donuts. He had a lot of questions he wanted answered. He'd been in the league for more than a decade and he wanted to know why I did things the way I did. But he wasn't belligerent; I interpreted his questions as a guy genuinely trying to figure out where I was coming from.

Things eventually got better between us, but that

didn't happen overnight. To create trust with people, talk is cheap, and the only thing that matters is how you act toward them over a long period of time. Over the next several years, Michael realized that I wasn't the maniac the writers made me out to be in Jacksonville. In fact, he'd later say my practices were the *least* physical of any of the coaches he'd been around. As we came to understand each other, we realized we had similar core values. Michael has said that he came to a crossroads where he realized he had to either be part of the disease or part of the cure. He bought in, and over the years my respect for the player and leader kept growing.

All of that preceded training camp in 2007. Michael had missed about half the season before with a foot injury and was unsure of whether or not he wanted to come back. He stayed in shape, but as training camp went on, he remained on the fence about whether or not he'd play. Michael was thirty-six years old by then, and as football players get older, it becomes more and more challenging for them to get themselves ready for a season. Michael had no shortage of postfootball opportunities to jump into, and he wasn't sure if he was committed to putting the work in to meet his own high standards.

I obviously wanted him back—but only if his heart was in it. I had too much respect for him to pressure him into doing something. But what I *could* do was to stay in touch with him, to tell him what we were building for that season, to appeal to something that is at the core of his identity despite his many talents: his sense of being a teammate. At least once a week, I called him and brought him up to speed on what was happening in camp. The team, which had been left for dead in 2006, saw the upcoming season as a tremendous challenge. I knew Michael would want to take that challenge on.

Finally, five days before our opening game, Michael decided to come back. He was in tip-top shape (although it takes a few weeks of getting knocked around to be in *football* shape). A couple of days after his return, our team voted to determine who our captains would be. Michael was a unanimous choice.

———

For Michael and his fellow defensive linemen, Super Bowl XLII was legacy defining. Michael is a Hall of Famer, of course, and in the Giants' Ring of Honor, he's joined by Osi and Justin. They would have been star players without Super Bowl XLII but it enriches their careers to have a single game that captures their greatness. When people think of them, they can focus on this one moment in time when they were too much for the Patriots' offensive line, when they battered Tom Brady and ground that explosive offense to a halt. It makes me proud that they will be remembered in this game as teammates, doing it together.

What those guys did in that game had its origins in the defensive line room at our facility. The energy in that room was *unique*. It was by far the loudest and most rambunctious room. Aggressive, not for the faint of heart. I'd walk by and hear the guys hooting and hollering, laughing and yelling and getting on one another's asses. Usually I'd walk right on by, not wanting to know too much about what was going on. I knew enough: That room generated the energy that powered our team.

In that room, you'd better be on your toes at all times, because there were a bunch of aggressive, high-achieving guys with sharp wits. If they were watching film of a practice and they saw you jogging, they'd jump all over you—and then fine you. If you missed a tackle in a game, or it was obvious you didn't know your assignment, they'd do the same thing. *Nothing* was missed: They had a dry-erase board where they kept track of the fines, week by week. It created a demanding sense of accountability. Maximum effort was mandatory in that room.

That was all Michael's influence. He taught those guys how to work and how to approach the game, which is another reason why someone like Michael is so valuable: It's not just his own work ethic, it's his impact on younger guys, and how that work ethic gets passed down through the generations.

His original protégé was Osi, and those guys formed quite a duo. While Michael was high-energy and outgoing, Osi's personality balanced him out. He was Mr. Cool, with a little shuffle to his walk, leaned over to one side a little bit. His parents were Nigerian and he'd been born in London, then moved back to Nigeria before heading to Alabama. He was one of five siblings, and everything about his demeanor reflected a confidence that he could relate to and get along with everybody. He always spoke in a measured, eloquent way. Like Michael, he had once been overweight but had worked himself into great shape. His calm demeanor balanced out Michael's exuberance.

As a right defensive end, he was your prototypical modern pass rusher. He was lean and exceptionally quick. Even before he established himself, Ernie Accorsi knew what he had in Osi and refused to include him as part of the 2004 draft day trade that brought us Eli. Ernie's faith would be rewarded soon after, culminating on the September night in 2007 when Osi set the single-game sack record against the Eagles, sacking Donovan McNabb six times.

Osi played by instinct—and had an innate nose for the ball, which he showed when he recovered

Brady's fumble to close out the first half. It's the type of thing you can't teach: Sometimes, he'd swat the ball out of the quarterback's hand without even touching the quarterback.

He was eager to learn from Michael, and he picked up his practice and study habits. In particular, Michael taught him how to anticipate snap counts to get a split-second jump off the line of scrimmage on key plays, like Michael's sack of Brady on the drive to open the second half.

Another thing that Michael taught Osi: taking pride in stopping the run. In practice, they competed with each other to see who could touch the ballcarrier first. You'd see these things in practice, then you'd see Osi stop a key third-down run on the Patriots' second series. One thing didn't happen without the other.

———

Of course, nobody made more big plays in Super Bowl XLII than Justin Tuck. Sometimes it's just your night, and this was Justin's. Justin had always been a talented player, but that game set him on the path for what he'd become: an all-time great New York Giant whose name is on MetLife Stadium's Ring of Honor.

Justin was a good fit for the Giants and the type

of person the organization has always wanted to employ. He was smart and well-rounded, and could talk about things other than football. An *adult*. A traditional guy who married his college sweetheart. A guy who grew up in a tiny town in Alabama and came from a large family—there are Tucks all over that town—who left for Notre Dame and then made it in the big city on the biggest stage, who now works for Goldman Sachs, a degree from Wharton in hand. He had a polished presence about him from the moment he entered the league. But he also had respect for tradition, so all the ribbing he took from Strahan and the veterans, all the times he had to get food for them on Fridays when they watched film together, he handled in stride with a sly smile.

As a defensive end, he was quick and powerful, good at pinning the outside arm of the offensive lineman he was going against and then lowering his shoulder to get leverage. When Michael retired, he moved to the left defensive end spot opposite Osi, and when Osi left as a free agent, he moved to the right side. But in the 2007 postseason, and the Super Bowl, he was quick and powerful enough to rush *inside*, enabling us to pit him against guards who couldn't match him athletically.

He came to us with an injury history at Notre Dame, which meant that he slid down to the third round of the draft. But it was obvious early on he was a first-round talent, and his talent forced us to get him on the field. With our NASCAR package, we were able to do that.

One of the things I really respected about Justin was that you could be direct and confrontational with him and he'd hear you out and take it in, even if it was something he didn't want to hear. In 2011, late in the season he was battling through some injuries, and his frustration began to show in his body language. I called him into my office and told him that he was a respected veteran the other guys took cues from. As a leader, I said, he had the opportunity to push past his frustration and lead by example. He took it to heart, and from that point on he stepped up his game. I remember him being on the practice field ten minutes early, chirping *Let's go, Coach!* with that smile of his, showing me he was ready.

It culminated with another outstanding postseason and Super Bowl win. For those two postseasons, it would be hard for any Giant, from any decade, to compete with how productive Justin was. He was historically good, and that's his legacy. Like Eli Manning, he played his best when the stakes were highest. That's why those guys have two Super Bowl rings each.

Justin is now well established in the corporate world, where he's a great ambassador for the Jay

Fund. Strahan is a television star who's been on the cover of *People* magazine. Osi married Miss Universe in 2011—literally!—and now lives in London, where he covers the NFL for the BBC, straddling worlds as always. His latest project is leading a developmental program in Africa to promote American football and cultivate talent. This is an incredibly impressive group of people. These guys are achievers. It's no coincidence they powered the defensive line that led us to the greatest win in Super Bowl history.

———

Throughout the second and third quarters, the Patriots kept getting the ball with the chance to go up by two scores. We kept stopping them. Maybe for most people watching, there was the belief that Brady would figure out our defense eventually, that the dam would break, that the Patriots would start to roll like they had all season. But we didn't think that. Our front four kept winning. Our blitzes kept getting there.

On the first play of the Patriots' first drive of the second half, Steve dialed up another blitz involving Antonio and Kawika, resulting in a tipped pass by Kawika that *almost* led to an interception that could've been brought back for a touchdown. But football is a game of inches, something the rest of the game would illustrate.

The Patriots strung together some good plays after that, managing three first downs on that drive. But our defense stiffened around midfield and got a stop, thanks in part to another unsuccessful deep shot to Moss, which was foiled, in part, because Justin once again hit Brady.

On the first play of the fourth quarter, Patriots punter Chris Hanson knocked a touchback through the end zone, giving us the ball on the 20. Through three quarters, the defense had been fantastic. Now it was the offense's turn.

Chapter Six

WHERE I COME FROM, WHO I AM

For me, the road to the fourth quarter of Super Bowl XLII began in Waterloo, New York.

Waterloo is in the Finger Lakes region of the state, about 225 miles northwest of New York City. It's situated on a twenty-mile barge canal that connects Cayuga Lake to Seneca Lake, and links those bodies of water to the Erie Canal. Formed in 1829, Waterloo exists because it was home to a set of "locks" on the barge canal, which regulated the flow of water.

It was that system of waterways that drew my family to the area. My maternal grandfather, Jay Post, who came from Canada, helped build the barge canal. The brother of my paternal grandmother, who came from Ireland, was a riverboat captain on the Erie Canal.

Waterloo was designated the birthplace of Memorial Day in 1966 by President Lyndon B. Johnson; a century before, the village held the nation's first-ever remembrance for the Civil War dead. Growing up, we knew that history, and we were raised with a respect for patriotism and service. It was typical Small Town USA, and its values became my values. I was an altar boy at St. Mary's Catholic Church and played sports year-round, mostly football, basketball, and baseball. We'd go swimming in the canal, where the water was cold and crisp and beautiful and clean. It was a great place to be a kid, and I consider myself very lucky to have grown up there.

My hometown shaped me, and so did my family. The importance of structure, dependability, and looking out for one another came from growing up in a four-bedroom, one-bath house with ten people: me, my five younger siblings, my parents, and my maternal grandparents. (My sixth sibling, my sister Chris, was born when I was sixteen.) We shared bedrooms and took turns in the bathroom. Everyone had to be up at a certain time and home for dinner by five thirty, and then we stayed quiet in the evening so my grandfather could get his sleep. Everyone did jobs around the house. We depended on one another.

We didn't have much in the way of extra money, and there were times growing up when we didn't have a car. There was no wiggle room, yet somehow everything *worked*—there was always food on the table and the house was full of love. It worked because of structure, discipline, work ethic, and selflessness. Those values are very precious to me, and when I became a coach, I wanted to instill them in my teams.

My dad, John Louis "Lou" Coughlin (which is pronounced "CAWK-lin" up in Waterloo) was "Old Irish," as they say. He was decent and kind, but like all men of that time and place, he was firm and no-nonsense, and wasn't afraid to take off his belt if we got out of line. He had a really good sense of humor, but you had to work to get him there. When he came out of the service after World War II he immediately got a job at the Seneca Army Depot, where ammunition was stored, and he had good benefits even though he never made a lot of money. He loved sports—baseball and soccer were his favorites—and we used to play catch in the yard. In sports as in life, he made clear there was only one way to do things: the right way.

He came from that generation of men where a father's love for his kids, and the sacrifices he makes for them, are obvious but not spoken about. Compliments were hard to come by. When I got older and excelled in sports, he was supportive, but I can't recall him ever saying "Great game!" or patting me

on the back. There was a football game in my sophomore year of high school, which was my first year
playing organized ball after an injury took me out
of freshman year, when I had played *decently* but not
great. I'd been distracted all game and didn't give
my best—which didn't escape my dad's notice.

When I came home and began to open the front
door, my dad was standing in the doorway.

—*If that's as hard as you're gonna play*, he said, *you
might wanna find something else to do with your time.*

I didn't argue with him because I knew he was
right, and in those days you didn't think about talking back. It was an example of tough love. It might
not have felt great at the time, but I never doubted it
was love.

My mom, Betty, was extremely warm, with an
outgoing personality. She was very proper in her
comportment and expected the same from us. She
emphasized basic morals: *Your word is your bond.
You're responsible for your behavior.* She was kind, but
not soft. If the nuns at school ever had a problem
with us, there was no pleading our case with her.

My mom treated everybody with respect regardless of their stature and was comfortable around all
types of people. She could be with the owner of the
New York Giants or Jacksonville Jaguars, and she
was the same person she was around service workers. Obviously she was never a rich woman—when

I was in high school, she took a job in the school cafeteria—but she always carried herself with a kind of regal pride. There was something so dignified and statuesque about the way she'd sit, with her hands clasped together, perched on the front part of her chair with good posture. When I see my daughter Keli in a meeting for the Jay Fund, for which she serves as CEO, I see my mother.

With her warmth, my mother took after her own mom, my maternal grandmother, Sarah Post, who lived in the house with us and filled it with her generous spirit. She was famous around town for her "fry cakes"—an Upstate New York fried dough specialty—and she and I had a unique bond. She taught me how to play euchre, and some of my best childhood memories are of playing that card game with her. Picture a cold winter night, with snow up to your rear end. We eat dinner, and then my grandmother says to me, *Would you like to play some euchre?* and we'd spend the rest of the night playing and talking, just the two of us.

She'd had some serious hardships in life, losing a young son, Freddie, to scarlet fever and then losing my uncle Ken at forty-one to an infection. Those moments left their scars—I remember her crying when she'd talk about Freddie—but she maintained an incredible ability to enjoy life. She had a great big laugh, and she always found little ways to make life fun. When she'd bake pies, for instance, she'd spell the names of me or my siblings in the dough.

She had a stroke when I was in college, and my parents didn't tell me about it because they wanted to *keep the bad news away from me*, which was what people said and thought at the time, with the best of intentions. I came home during my senior year when the town of Waterloo honored me by hosting a Tom Coughlin Day, and I'll never forget walking into my childhood home and seeing my grandmother in the condition she was in. It gutted me.

Grandparents were an integral part of my upbringing. My maternal grandfather, a construction laborer, could do absolutely everything with his hands: He built his own bed, and you would've sworn it was a luxury product he'd ordered from a furniture catalog.

My paternal grandparents lived nearby in Waterloo. My paternal grandmother, Eleanor "Nellie" Coughlin, had a great sense of humor and was whip-smart. Her husband, John Francis Coughlin, had been a night watchman on the railroad. Like his wife, he had a dry Irish wit. All my grandparents were always very accepting of us. When we'd mess up, our parents would mete out the discipline. Our grandparents' job was to provide a foundation of love.

———

I was the oldest of my siblings—we were two boys, five girls—and consequently there were expectations on me, which I took to heart. These expectations helped form my identity: I was the responsible one, the serious one. From the time I was twelve, I delivered groceries on a bike. I mowed lawns and shoveled snow for widows, a dollar per lawn or driveway. If I wanted to buy a soda with my friends, I'd have to earn that money. This made sense to me on a basic level. The principle of work before play was something I embraced. It seemed obvious to me that that was how the world should work.

My brother John was a character, the one with the gregarious charm who knew everyone in town. My paternal grandfather trained horses, and sometimes he'd pick my brother up from school and tell the teachers he had a dentist appointment, but instead they'd go to the track. But horse racing wasn't my thing. The few times I went, I'd get antsy, and I'd run laps around the track.

Just like at home, structure and discipline reigned at school. My elementary school was run by the Sisters of St. Joseph. If my players with the Giants thought I ran a tight ship, they'd never been around those nuns. You sat up straight, you raised your hand a certain way, and when the bell rang, you went out of the classroom in a neat, single-file line. Because space and resources were tight, each classroom housed two grades, with one nun teaching both. You listened to the nuns and followed the rules, and when they took out the ruler, nobody batted an eye. Everyone knew it was done to keep us on task.

Church had that same structure, and the structure, tradition, and hierarchy of the Catholic Church was very meaningful to me. The church bound our community together, but it also connected us to the wider world beyond Waterloo. Church was a place that rewarded you for doing the right thing, and I gravitated to that idea and became an altar boy. I was extremely honored at being selected as master of ceremonies for both the Christmas and Easter midnight masses in seventh and eighth grade. It's hard to overstate how important those types of honors were in a small community like Waterloo.

And to be clear, *nothing* was above the church in terms of importance. Picture this scene: I'm in sixth grade, in math class, and the priest comes to the door of my classroom and delivers the news: Someone has died, and I have to do a funeral mass.

No questions asked, I'm out of my seat. Within a few minutes I'm in my cassock and surplice and I'm lighting candles.

Maybe that was why I was such a lousy math student.

———

Sports were huge in my hometown, a way our community organized itself. There was a tremendous sense of pride about sports and the values they could embody. When we got into high school, we felt that as athletes, we represented our town—not just in terms of winning and losing, but in how we comported ourselves.

Of course, I gravitated toward athletics from an early age. Basketball, football, baseball—sports organized everything in my life. I loved the competition, I loved being surrounded by my friends, I loved leading my team, I loved succeeding. As a kid I'd devour author Clair Bee's series of books about the character Chip Hilton: The basic premise is that Hilton, the hero, urges his teammates in basketball, football, and baseball to do their best on the field and to demonstrate their best character, including in the classroom. He always succeeds, and the team always wins.

I held the idea of competition as something sacred; I've always believed there's no substitute for competition when it comes to bringing out the best in people. I remember being a grammar school kid when they taught us how to play basketball at the community rec center, and nobody really knew how to dribble or shoot. But we wanted to win, so we learned and refined those skills. We were driven to improve by competition.

The first great team I was ever on was my grammar school basketball team. We were 25-0, but we lost the championship game—it was a painful but powerful lesson. Still, there was a sense of excitement around town about what our group would accomplish when we got older, and in my junior and senior years of high school, our Waterloo High team won back-to-back sectionals in basketball. Our archrival in basketball was Lyons High School, whose best player my sophomore year was a senior who could shoot the lights out named Jim Boeheim. A few years later, Jim became my resident advisor at Syracuse.

In football, our Waterloo team won the Wayne–Finger Lakes Football Conference championship my junior and senior years. Later on in my life, I'd go down New York City's Canyon of Heroes twice in a float, but in terms of what it meant to the community, nothing topped the feeling of winning our local league in high school.

To clinch the title our junior year, we beat Mynderse Academy in Seneca Falls, a team that had beaten us eleven times in a row and had tormented us for decades. The game took place at our home field, which was a short drive from our school. (They've since built a small stadium at the school, named Tom Coughlin Stadium.) We beat Mynderse 27–0, and when we returned to our school gym after the game to turn in our equipment, a bunch of guys in their twenties and thirties who'd played for Waterloo were there to greet the team and celebrate with us. You felt the way sports could connect people through generations: *Our* win was *their* win.

After we got changed in the locker room, we went downtown, where it seemed like everyone in Waterloo was there and going crazy. It was my first inkling of how winning a championship can make everyone in a community stand a little taller.

The coaches of my youth were some of the most influential people in my life. They're still towering figures for me, the model for how coaches can instill values and mold young people. A lot of teenagers are directionless, but I was lucky: By junior year of high school, I knew I wanted to be a football coach.

My high school football coach, Mike Ornato, was twenty-six when he became our head coach. We loved him, and he went on to a long, storied career, eventually moving on to Greenwich High School in Connecticut, where he taught Steve Young the intricacies of quarterback play. At Waterloo, the young and charismatic coach would regale us with stories from his time in the Army a few years before.

Bill Carey, my basketball coach, was a sharp-tongued Irish guy—the type of coach who carried a volleyball around and would fire it inches above our heads if we weren't paying attention. He was tough but extremely caring, a mentor I could talk to about anything and everything. We stayed close when I went off to college, and our friendship has grown in the years since.

It was Coach Carey who used his connections to place the call that landed me my first head coaching job at Division III Rochester Institute of Technology. He'd always been a huge Giants fan, so when I became the Giants' head coach, I'd have him at training camp in Albany and bring him to games, where he'd sit in the box with my wife, Judy. As my career progressed, I carried a piece of him with me, just like I did with many of my coaches.

I loved all sports, but football was my favorite. The magic of the Saturday afternoon football game was unique: I remember being a little kid and going to the field and peeking through the fence with my friends, because it cost a dollar to get in. I didn't play organized football until high school, but we had always played in the backyard, and from day one I loved the excitement of running with the ball and making people miss. When I started playing with helmets and pads, I liked it even more. I loved watching the hole open up and the challenge of bursting through it before it closed. I loved lowering a shoulder in anticipation of contact. I loved the contact itself.

Football is the greatest team sport that was ever invented. A lot of people don't like it because it's *hard*—but that was exactly what I loved so much about it. It rewarded preparation, teamwork, and selflessness. It was consistent with everything I was taught about what's truly valuable: You pay a great price, but the greater the price, the greater the reward. If something wasn't difficult, there was no value in attaining it.

———

Growing up in Upstate New York, I never wanted to play college football anywhere but Syracuse— a powerhouse that had won the National Championship in 1959. I'd watched Coach Schwartzwalder's Thursday night coaching show growing up, and I'd idolized Jim Brown and Ernie Davis—in high school, my teammates called me "Ernie" because he was a running back and so was I. When it came time for college, I was extremely grateful that Syracuse was one of the small handful of schools that recruited me. (Another school was Buffalo; a young assistant named Buddy Ryan came to Waterloo and sat in my living room with my parents.)

Although I was my team's primary ballcarrier in high school, one look at the Syracuse roster made it obvious that wouldn't be the case there: Ahead of me on the depth chart in the backfield were Floyd Little and Larry Csonka, both future NFL Hall of Famers, along with Jim Nance, who was a two-time NCAA wrestling champion before going on to a pro football career. But that didn't diminish my interest in playing there. I was captivated by the school's tradition and I took pride in being a team guy, so I worked on my blocking and put on some muscle so I could transition to wingback, which was primarily a blocking position with the occasional "Syracuse Scissors"—a misdirection inside run—mixed in. By the end of my sophomore year, I started the last two games at wingback, partnered in the backfield with Floyd and Larry.

We were a tough, physical running team in the mold of our head coach. About a decade before he volunteered for World War II as a thirty-two-year-old paratrooper, Coach Schwartzwalder had been a 150-pound center at the University of West Virginia, so he appreciated that football games were won and lost in the trenches, and with toughness. He wasn't much for rah-rah speeches because for him actions spoke louder than words. I appreciated that about him—one of my favorite expressions when I became a coach was: *Talk is cheap. Play the game.*

He was also extremely *loyal.* If you worked hard and showed good character, you'd be in his good graces, considered one of "Ben's boys." I admired the way he quietly inspired us to be the best we could be.

Early on at Syracuse, the PA addresser would always butcher my name and refer to me as "COCK-lin," a mispronunciation of "CAWK-lin"—and I wasn't about to let that stand. To make things easier, I asked my paternal grandmother if she'd mind if I pronounced my name the way it was spelled— "COFF-lin"—and after I got her blessing, I told the people at Syracuse to say it that way. It's been that way ever since.

During my last two years at Syracuse, we won eight games each year, including a win to close out my senior year against number four–ranked UCLA, led by Heisman Trophy winner Gary Beban. I was hardly a star, but I made a contribution, setting a then record for receptions during my senior year with twenty-six. That's something I love about football: If you're a team-oriented person, willing to do whatever it takes to contribute, there's likely a place for you.

After college, I knew I wanted to be a football coach, and I knew you had to start on the bottom. First was being a graduate assistant at Syracuse while I got my master's degree in secondary education. (I'd always worked hard at school: In college I won the Orange Key Award, given to a student-athlete who'd demonstrated commitment to their studies.) The next year brought my first paid job, as an assistant at Rochester Institute of Technology. The following year I was promoted to head coach, and while it might have been DIII, it was a tremendous responsibility for a guy in his early twenties. I was responsible for *everything* that happened in that program: scheduling games, making hotel and bus arrangements, and recruiting players—which consisted mostly of walking around campus and trying to convince the big kids that football was fun.

I was twenty-three when I took the job, and it was sink or swim: I didn't know what I was doing but I had to figure it out, to grow up fast in the profession. And I did. Those three years at RIT were incredibly important to my development. Nearly a quarter century later, when I became the first head coach of the Jacksonville Jaguars, my first NFL head coaching job, I drew heavily on that experience. From the humble beginnings of operating an NFL franchise out of a trailer in the mud, starting with players other NFL teams didn't want, we made the playoffs four times in my first five years and went to two AFC Championship games. I'm extremely proud of what we did in Jacksonville, and I couldn't have done it without my time at RIT.

In between RIT and becoming an NFL head coach? I mostly did what all up-and-coming coaches did: I bounced around from assistant job to assistant job, working with some great people with different styles, absorbing everything I could.

Syracuse, under Frank Maloney, who was mentored by Bo Schembechler—I was the quarterbacks and running backs coach and then got promoted to offensive coordinator. Boston College, under Jack Bicknell, where I was Doug Flutie's quarterbacks coach. The Philadelphia Eagles, under Marion Campbell, who gave me my break in the NFL, where I was the wide receivers coach and worked with innovative offensive minds like Sid Gillman and Ted Marchibroda. Green Bay, under the great Forrest Gregg, who played under Vince Lombardi— I was the wide receivers coach and came to love Green Bay, which had small-town values like Waterloo and was steeped in football history.

A lot of life happened during all these stops. In 1969, my grad assistant year at Syracuse, Judy gave birth to our first child, Keli Ann. Then came Timothy Paul in 1972, Brian Thomas in 1977, and Kathleen Elizabeth in 1981. (I'll talk about Judy and my family a little later.) Being a young coach can be tough on a family, and in 1980, after Frank Maloney resigned from the Syracuse job, I thought about changing careers into something more stable, like selling insurance. But Judy, in her quiet way, encouraged me to follow my dreams: *Sure you're gonna sell insurance*, she'd say with a telling smile. I'm forever indebted to her for that and so much more.

My last stop as an assistant coach was East Rutherford, New Jersey, where of course we won the Super Bowl in 1990. But that season will always be bittersweet for me. That year, my father died of a heart attack at sixty-nine. He'd retired ten years before, but he'd battled health issues the whole time and was never really able to enjoy his retirement. He'd worked so hard and sacrificed so much, and then it seemed like he was gone, just like that. I remember being at his funeral and thinking, *Is this all there is?*

A few months later, we won Super Bowl XXV in Tampa, and being a part of that effort was a validation of everything I'd been working toward my entire adult life. I was confident about what I'd learned in all those years and with all those great coaches. I'd always told myself I wanted to be a head coach at a major program by the time I turned forty-five. Now it was time.

Right after the Super Bowl, I hit the recruiting trail as the new head coach at Boston College. I wasn't gonna let this opportunity go to waste. My focus was sharp and my methods, by that point in my career, were refined. I knew exactly what type of head coach I wanted to be and I set the tone early on.

My first day on campus, I went to an indoor facility to watch players do an off-season conditioning program. I just stood there for about twenty minutes and watched them without saying a word. Soon after, I spotted one player going to the bathroom in the middle of a drill. I followed him in there—and then I questioned his commitment and dragged him out. Then, knowing that BC had posted a losing record for five straight years, I addressed my team.

—*Guys, I promise you one thing*, I told them. *When you leave here, everything in your life is gonna be easier than this.*

My first year there, 1991, we went 4-7. But the next year we turned it around and went 8-3-1, finishing twenty-first in the final AP poll. During that 1992 season, the Giants reached out to me to gauge my interest in becoming their head coach the following year. But I wasn't yet two years into my time at BC, and my work there wasn't done, so I declined to pursue it further.

I felt a strong bond to the players and the school community. The Jesuit philosophy, in its commitment to morality and service, fit me to a T. I expected my players to dedicate themselves to their schoolwork as well as their football, which meant we had really good relationships with professors. Coaches, professors, and the high-quality caliber of kids we were recruiting—everyone was on the same page about important values, and I thrived in that environment.

Our bond was strengthened by tragedy—the 1992 death of Jay McGillis, one of my favorite players in all my years of coaching. Jay, a strong safety on our team, was an overachiever and a great teammate, a blue-collar kid from Brockton, Massachusetts, who was beloved by his teammates. In 1991, we were scheduled to play Miami, the number one team in the nation, when the doctors told me Jay would have to miss the game: He had swollen glands and was running a fever.

We didn't think much of it at the time, but the news took a sudden, awful turn: We learned Jay had leukemia—and a particularly aggressive form of it. The next few months were like a nightmare. I watched Jay become ravaged by that horrible disease, and I saw the emotional and financial toll it took on his family, who sat vigil by his bedside day after day. Their love and commitment to Jay was as honorable as it was heartbreaking. Jay died eight months after his diagnosis, on July 3, 1992.

But he did not die in vain. The charity I launched in Jay's honor in 1996, the Jay Fund Foundation, has provided more than $16 million to families tackling childhood cancer. Decades later, we're going strong. Every family and child we've helped knows Jay's story. It's an amazing thing to see.

At BC, our team was brought closer together by our shared loss. And I'm profoundly grateful that during that era, we won a high-profile game that people can remember that team by. It was 1993; our record was 7-2, and we were the seventeenth-ranked team in the country. We went into South Bend, Indiana, to play Notre Dame, the number one team in the land, who'd just beaten Florida State in a matchup between unbeaten powerhouses dubbed "the Game of the Century."

Notre Dame at that point had the inside track to the National Championship, and next up for them was us. In the only four meetings between the programs to that point, Notre Dame had beaten BC all four times, including a 54–7 blowout the previous year. Among their many scores was one that followed a fake punt called by Lou Holtz in the third quarter, when they already had a 37–0 lead.

We didn't forget that when we traveled to South Bend—a road game, because everyone knew Notre Dame wouldn't travel to play a school they considered beneath them. To hear everyone tell it, we were a speed bump on their road to a title.

But we believed in ourselves, and we came out motivated, and early in the fourth quarter, we had a 38–17 lead. But then Notre Dame stormed back, scoring twenty-two points in eleven minutes, taking a one-point lead with about a minute to go. I can imagine what most people were thinking: The great Notre Dame team had averted the upset. The *right team* would win the game.

But *we* were the right team. On our last drive, our fiery quarterback, Glenn Foley, drove us downfield, all the way to Notre Dame's 24-yard line with five seconds left. Our field goal team came out, and Foley, who was also our holder, knelt down at the 31-yard line to receive the snap.

The 31. I noted that number at the time. It was the jersey number of Jay McGillis.

We brought out David Gordon to kick the field goal—our left-footed, nonscholarship kicker, who over the past two seasons had missed his previous two attempts to win games with field goals. David's father was Richard Gordon, the owner of the NHL's Hartford Whalers at the time, who'd called me to let him know his son was going to BC and asked if he could try out as a kicker. David made the best of his opportunity—I can picture him going out on a snowy, ten-degree day and practicing field goals by himself—and now here he was, on NBC, with a chance to knock off the country's number one team.

Before he ran onto the field, the only thing I told David was to focus on hitting the ball squarely.

And he did. But for a moment it looked like the ball would go wide right—until it made a screwball-like turn and went through the uprights straight down the middle.

Did Jay McGillis have something to do with the path of that ball?

Pandemonium on our side ensued. I ran to the middle of the field and shook hands with Lou Holtz, and then did a quick interview with NBC's John Dockery, who asked if this was a *revenge game* from last year, to which I said, *No*.

Then I ran into the locker room. The only people who were there were myself and Father J. Donald Monan, BC's president. The players were still out on the field, celebrating with the large contingent of fans who'd traveled from Massachusetts.

Nearly thirty years later, people still come up to me and tell me where they were when David Gordon kicked that field goal.

Tell the 1993 Boston College Eagles they couldn't do something.

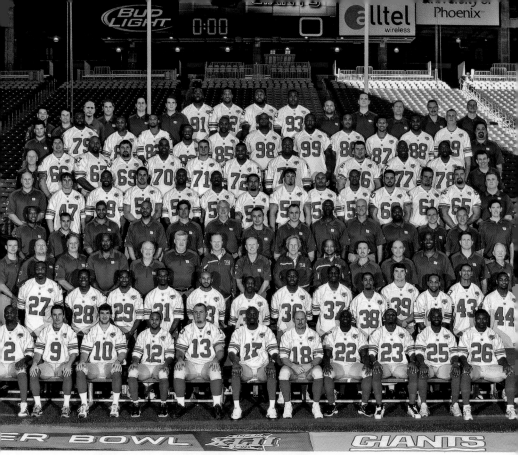

The New York Giants, 2007 Super Bowl champions.

In the week leading up to the game, I had a feeling of peace about our team's mindset and preparation. I was confident we were up to the challenge.

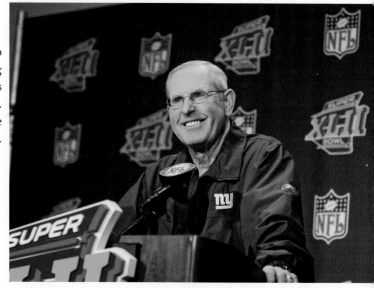

We enjoyed our week in Arizona, while keeping focused on the task at hand. The Friday before the game, we had a team family picnic, and all the families took hayrides there.

Michael Strahan is the greatest natural leader I've ever been around. Here, he's pumping up his teammates before the Super Bowl.

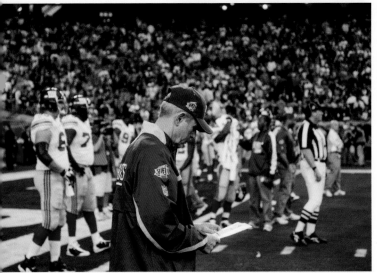

Minutes before kickoff, I'm making sure we're on schedule with our pregame routine.

We might have been underdogs, but we were confident. We'd faced lots of adversity, but now we were exactly where we wanted to be.

Our pass rush dominated the game, and Justin Tuck had one of the greatest Super Bowls a defensive player has ever had.

When I hired Steve Spagnuolo before the 2007 season, I was drawn by his aggressive approach and his positive energy.

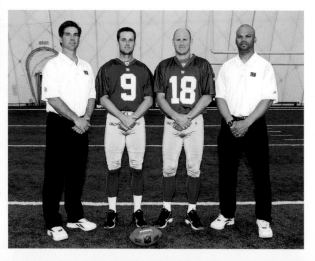

Our special teams coordinator, Tom Quinn, and assistant coordinator, Thomas McGaughey, along with Lawrence Tynes and Jeff Feagles.

Our offensive line was the foundation of our offense. They were a bunch of tough, high-character guys, coached by Pat Flaherty.

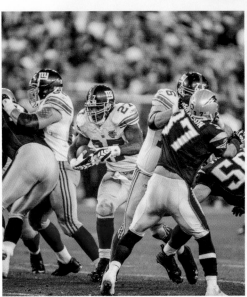

Brandon Jacobs and Ahmad Bradshaw were close friends whose running styles complemented each other perfectly.

Kevin Boss was one of many Giants rookies in 2007 who played like a veteran. His 45-yard catch and run to start the fourth quarter jump-started our offense.

On David Tyree's famous Helmet Catch play, Eli Manning broke tackle attempts by two defensive linemen. A lesser competitor would have gone down.

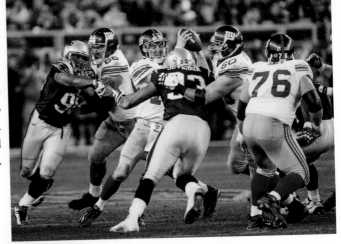

There are four Vince Lombardi Trophies at Giants team headquarters. Kevin Gilbride, who doesn't get nearly enough credit, called every offensive play for two of them.

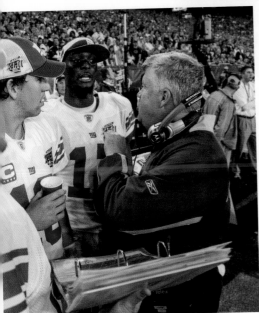

Just before our go-ahead touchdown, Eli Manning told Plaxico Burress that if he was in single coverage, the ball would come his way.

Eli Manning, two-time Super Bowl MVP, should be a slam-dunk Hall of Famer.

My daughter Kate with her husband, Chris Snee, and my grandson Dylan.

Each of the studio analysts at Fox picked us to lose each game of the 2007 playoffs. Here I am, accepting the Vince Lombardi Trophy.

Celebrating on the field with my wife, Judy, and my daughter Keli. Michael Strahan has said, "Thank God for Judy. If there was no Judy, there'd be no Super Bowls."

Going down the Canyon of Heroes in a float was a bucket-list experience I'll never forget. We felt the power and energy of New York City—and the love New Yorkers have for their Giants.

Super Bowl XLII binds us at the hip for the rest of our lives.

When David Tyree reenacted his instantly famous Helmet Catch at our Giants Stadium reception, the crowd went wild.

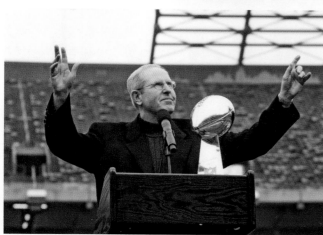

I've always been a "What's next?" kind of guy. So after our celebration at Giants Stadium, which capped off a day of adulation, I went to the dentist.

Life in the NFL goes on. You don't get back to the mountaintop by standing still. When one mission is accomplished, another is just beginning.

Chapter Seven

KEVIN BOSS AND THE ROOKIE BRIGADE TO THE RESCUE

By the fourth quarter of Super Bowl XLII, the 2007 Giants had a chance for a similar upset. We'd made big stops on defense all night. On offense, we'd moved the ball effectively at times but had only that field goal on our first drive to show for it. Down 7–3 at the start of the period, we needed a play. We got one from a guy who, at the beginning of the year, would have seemed like an unlikely source.

Kevin Boss was a rookie fifth-round draft pick, selected to provide depth behind our heralded tight end, Jeremy Shockey. Kevin had gone to a small, Division II school, Western Oregon, so he wasn't as pro-ready as guys from bigger schools, and his combine numbers didn't jump out at you. But make no mistake: Kevin was an athlete. At six foot seven, he'd played on his college basketball team, and his coordination and fluid movements were evident from the beginning.

We'd always liked him as a receiver, but he needed to develop as a blocker. Given how much our offense stressed the run, tight ends who couldn't block simply couldn't play—it was a similar principle as with running backs who couldn't pick up the blitz. For most of the regular season, Kevin didn't play much, but he kept his head down and worked hard on his blocking, becoming very competent. In football, you never know when you'll get your opportunity, but Kevin had worked his way into being ready for his—which came when Jeremy broke his leg in our fourteenth game, ending his season. The injury was a blow because of how talented Jeremy was. But we'd seen Kevin improve steadily, and he was ready to step in.

After he became a starter, it was obvious that Kevin and Eli had really good chemistry. It helped that he was so tall and long-limbed, with a height and reach advantage over any linebacker or safety. But just as important were his smooth, athletic movements: The passing game and route running are all about timing and rhythm. The more fluid the receiver is, the easier it is for the quarterback to be in sync with him—to be able to read when he's breaking so he can deliver a well-timed, well-placed ball. With a herky-jerky guy, things get out of rhythm, the timing gets out of whack, and a quarterback has a harder time anticipating when to release the ball.

Which brings us to the first play of the fourth quarter of Super Bowl XLII. We had just taken possession on our 20, on a touchback from a Patriots punt. We had been maintaining run-pass balance all game, and even though we hadn't been particularly successful on the ground—we'd averaged 3.9 yards on our eighteen running plays—staying balanced came with hidden advantages. This became apparent on that play, when, off a play-action fake that drew the linebackers toward the line of scrimmage, Eli hit Kevin twenty yards downfield, and then Kevin shook a tackle to run for a 45-yard gain, showing off the speed he possessed once his long strides got going. It was the longest play of the game for either team. We were at the Patriots' 35-yard line.

Just like that, we were in position to score our first points since the game's opening drive. Just like that, the energy in the building changed. Up to that point, on our five drives, we'd been in Patriots territory four times, including first downs at the Patriots' 17-, 19-, 31-, and 45-yard lines. We'd knocked on this door a bunch of times but hadn't broken through, but we were persistent and confident that *this* time, we'd capitalize on our chance and reach the end zone.

The play call that resulted in Kevin's catch had a pretty simple design. There were two backs, two wide receivers, and Kevin was the tight end on the right side. But it had a little wrinkle: Before the snap, Kevin went in what we call a "peel motion," which placed him five feet wide of right tackle Kareem McKenzie rather than the standard three feet. The motion allowed Kevin to get his momentum going forward; it gave him a clean release and a little more room to maneuver on the perimeter.

On Kevin's side, our wide receiver Steve Smith ran an out pattern, which took the cornerback on that side out of the play. On the other side, Plaxico Burress was getting double-covered by a corner-back and a safety. (Plaxico's stat line in that Super Bowl may not have been impressive, but the impact of having a guy like him on the field goes beyond his personal stats.) This meant that the middle of the field was open—and the play called for Kevin to read the deep-middle-third to determine if there was a safety there.

Since there wasn't, Kevin's job was simple: He was to make it *seem* like he was running toward the pylon, only to break into the open space in the middle of the field. That's exactly what he did, with a smooth, efficient move that created separation from

Patriots safety Rodney Harrison, who had picked up Kevin in man coverage.

The play action had sucked up the linebackers, giving Eli a clean lane to fire a perfect pass that hit Kevin in stride as he came out of his break to the inside. And Kevin, being the natural athlete that he is, didn't slow down even a fraction of a stride to catch the ball, which allowed him to break Harrison's tackle attempt and get an additional fifteen yards.

The play might have looked like a pretty simple pitch-and-catch, but that said something about the connection Eli had developed with Kevin, a guy who made things look easier than they were.

And now this rookie, who'd stepped up for us at just the right time, had completely swung the momentum of the game in a matter of seconds. The 18-0 Patriots were on their heels.

———

Three plays later: Another rookie, another big catch.

Steve Smith and Kevin Boss were very different players, but they shared the common trait of having athleticism that wasn't captured on TV or in the scouting combine numbers. I talked earlier about Steve, and what a tragedy it was that his career was cut short. I also discussed the important reception he made to extend our opening drive on third down, which gave us the opportunity to get into field goal range. Here was another important catch, on third-and-four from the Patriots' 29: Steve caught a laser from Eli across the middle for a 17-yard gain.

On the play, Steve was lined up in the slot against nickelback Randall Gay. His route called for him to beat Gay to the inside, but this presented a challenge: The Patriots lined up in a form of a twenty-two-man coverage, which meant that Gay's responsibility was inside leverage on the slot receiver. In other words, to *not* get beaten inside.

This was a moment where we needed a guy to play above the X's and O's in the manner in which I always challenge our players. And Steve, on a route that made it difficult to get open against that particular coverage, did exactly that: At the top of his route, he gave Gay a head-and-shoulder fake to the outside. Gay bought it completely, which allowed Steve to snap *inside* of him and up the field.

Steve's move was lightning-quick, smooth, and perfectly in time with the design of the play—and Eli rifled it into him for a seventeen-yard gain, a fraction of a moment before the deep safety, Brandon Meriweather, practically made a missile out of himself and dove at Steve's legs. Steve absorbed the hit and held on to the ball, and then got up and stared down Gay, a rookie staring into the face of a four-year veteran who'd already won a Super Bowl. First-and-ten Giants, from the Patriots' 12-yard line.

That play showed it all when it came to Steve: the quickness, the savvy, the toughness, and the fact that, like many of our rookies in 2007, he wasn't backing down from anything, including this moment.

Speaking of which: Our rookies in 2007—Jerry Reese and everyone involved in the draft struck gold with that class. There were so many talented players, and even though some saw their careers derailed by injuries, many made huge contributions in '07. We would not have won the Super Bowl without them.

I've talked about Steve, Kevin, and Ahmad, but there were others:

Aaron Ross, our first-round pick out of Texas, who was sound, versatile, and *tough*—a guy who separated his shoulder in the Dallas playoff game and played through it, making a key third-down tackle on Marion Barber with his arm hanging out of its socket. He had a great rookie season and was a starter on our 2011 Super Bowl team as well.

Jay Alford, who became our short snapper on field goals and was part of our interior defensive line rotation. Jay was strong—physically and mentally. In the NFC Championship game in Green Bay, when we attempted a field goal to win the game at the end of regulation, Jay's bad snap—in minus-twenty-four-degree weather—led Lawrence Tynes to shank the kick wide. Everyone remembers that Lawrence bounced back from that miss to become the hero, but so did Jay. His snap on Lawrence's game winner in overtime was perfect. That says a lot about the guy.

Zak DeOssie: Smart, enthusiastic, and extremely popular in the locker room, Zak was the Giants' long snapper for thirteen years, becoming a respected fixture in the organization. He was a linebacker by trade and was a key contributor on the kickoff team, where he got to fly downfield and throw his body around, which was what he loved doing most of all. After Jeff Feagles retired following the 2009 season, Zak was the Giants' special teams captain until his own retirement after the 2019 season. His dad, Steve DeOssie, had been a linebacker on our 1990 team, and now, both father and son are big supporters of the Jay Fund. They're both good men, both with Super Bowl rings, and it's something else to see how life comes full circle.

Michael Johnson, a seventh-round pick out of Arizona, whose great attitude and football instincts landed him in the starting lineup for five games during his rookie year. For the two years after that, he was a full-time starter for us. In the fourth quarter of the NFC Championship game, with the score tied, we fumbled on a punt return and a Packer player fell on top of it. But Michael alertly punched the ball from that player, allowing us to recover and maintain possession. That play summed up our rookie class: They made contributions all over the field, and they were always there when we needed them.

Including the guy we drafted twenty-six slots after Michael in the seventh round: Ahmad Bradshaw. I've talked about Ahmad's toughness and his ability to get low and grind out tough yards. On the play after Steve's catch, Ahmad's decisive, physical running put us on the doorstep of a touchdown.

It came on a draw play from a four-wide-receiver set, which spread out their defenders and gave Ahmad room to maneuver. This draw, from that formation, was a big play for us during my time in New York, showing again our commitment to balance and keeping the defense guessing: Even when we spread the field, the possibility of a run always existed.

On this play, on first-and-ten from the 12, Ahmad took the handoff and followed the inside shoulder of right guard Chris Snee, who overwhelmed the great Junior Seau with his strength and drove him back. Ahmad was about four yards downfield before contact even came, and he finished the run strong like he always did, falling forward for a seven-yard gain, down to the Patriots' 5-yard line.

Then Ahmad got up and started jawing with Rodney Harrison and some other Patriots. The refusal to be intimidated, the bold knowledge that they *belonged*—that summed up our rookie class.

———

For Ahmad to have picked up seven yards, setting up a second-and-three, was huge: It meant that on the next down, the Patriots had to be ready for a run. That allowed us to call a play we'd put in during the previous week of practice—a play we could use only once, which relied on the element of surprise.

The presence of wide receiver David Tyree in a short-yardage situation signaled one thing to the opponent: *run*. David's strength was special teams, and while he was a very capable receiver, his best attribute from an offensive perspective was his ability to block from that position. A physical guy who relished the contact of the game, David was someone we'd often use in short-yardage situations to stick his nose in the scrum and clear out a linebacker or a safety.

The play we called, and that we'd been practicing, gave every indication of being a run: We lined up three wide receivers to spread the field a little bit, with David as the lone receiver on one side and two receivers on the other side. We motioned David from a wide position closer toward the tight end—which signaled to the other team that David was going to block the first defender inside of him lined up off the ball.

At the snap of the ball came a very deceptive play-action fake—where our linemen fired off the ball like it was a normal running play, and Richie Seubert even pulled from his left guard spot. In this way, it looked exactly like our power run, which was one of our signature plays in the ground game.

For his part, David ran directly toward the inside defender at the second level, safety James Sanders, as if he was going to block him. But instead, David slipped behind Sanders into an open area of the zone, heading on a diagonal for the goalpost.

As soon as Eli finished his fake handoff, and with the linebacker drawn toward the line of scrimmage by the play action, Eli put his back foot in the ground and threw a strike to David, who caught it with his hands, face-high. The timing was just right, as it had been on Eli's two previous completions on this drive: Safety Brandon Meriwether, who was on the other side of the play and sprinted toward David, *almost* got there in time to break up the play, but was a fraction of a second late.

10–7, Giants.

There's obviously a lot more to say about David Tyree later in this book. But something to note here is that on the Friday before the game, during David's awful practice when he was dropping everything thrown in his direction, we practiced this play—and David dropped it.

But Eli had told him to shake it off, that he knew we could rely on him when it mattered. He had been proven right.

For the moment, we were happy to have the lead for the first time since the first quarter. When we scored, that building got loud, one of the many reminders that night that it was a pro-Giants crowd. The American public might have been surprised that the Giants were leading the undefeated Patriots in the fourth quarter, but we weren't. The big prize was visible before us: The entire season, our entire careers really, would come down to the next eleven minutes.

All of that was in the air. But there was only one thing going through my mind: *Stop Brady.*

Chapter Eight

HAIL TO THE ACHIEVERS

After David's touchdown, eleven minutes and ten seconds stood between us and a Super Bowl title.

Becoming a champion—that's what's pulling you forward all those years. From the moment you get into this profession, it's in the distance, but you keep grinding, you keep giving your best for all those long days. There were so many nights you slept on the office couch. There were so many nights you couldn't actually sleep, because a loss was gnawing at you. Then, all of a sudden, it's right in front of you. Your place in sports history.

Of course, I'm not thinking about any of this at the time. But I am aware that being so close raises the stakes. We *have* to win. Those of us who have spent our lives in sports know how rare these opportunities are.

I've often been asked who my favorite all-time athletes are. My answer to that is: *Who are the greatest champions?* Bill Russell is one name that pops into my head. Bill Russell means *championships*. Bill Russell embodied everything I've always preached to my players: If you play selflessly, if you do all the dirty work, if you put your team before yourself, you have a chance of winning championships. You are defined by your team's accomplishments.

To this day, I'm still in awe of men like Russell, who won eleven NBA Championships. Or Yogi Berra, who won ten World Series in his playing career. Or John Wooden, who won ten NCAA titles over a twelve-year period. I've worked my whole adult life in sports, but at heart I'm a fan, too. No matter what you've accomplished, you still revere the great ones. My first sports hero was Jim Brown, who at Syracuse became the greatest college football player ever—and the greatest college lacrosse player ever—when I was just a little kid. He was followed at Syracuse by Ernie Davis, the first African American to win the Heisman Trophy, whose moves and mannerisms I emulated, leading to my high school nickname of "Ernie."

One of my favorite sayings is "Hail to the Achievers." I've always tried to communicate this to my teams: Our business is professional football, so we're going to be judged on success, and success means winning.

As a fourteen-year-old growing up in Upstate New York, I had the privilege of going to the 1961 NBA All-Star Game in Syracuse. The amount of talent on that floor that day was like a who's who of the greatest basketball players of all time: Oscar Robertson, Bob Cousy, Wilt Chamberlain, Bob Pettit, Elgin Baylor, Bill Russell himself.

As far as the history of football, and all who came before me—I have the utmost admiration for way too many people to list. Paul Brown was the first great coach I ever had any contact with: I was twelve years old and had just watched the Browns lose the NFL Championship game, and I was upset because I was a huge Jim Brown fan and I'd wanted the Browns to win. I wrote Paul Brown a letter about the game—and to my shock, he wrote back, sending me a nice note along with pictures of the team.

I was in awe of Coach Brown then, just as I am now. The late John Madden put it best when he said that he truly believed, with all his heart, that the busts in the Pro Football Hall of Fame talk to each other. I'm with him, and I'd give anything to be a fly on the wall listening to the conversations between the game's great coaches who are no longer with us, like Paul Brown, Vince Lombardi, Don Shula, Bill Walsh, and John himself.

As my career progressed, sports didn't lose that magic. In the early 1980s, I was in the Boston area as an assistant at BC when the Magic Johnson–Larry Bird rivalry was heating up, and I'd go to games at the old Boston Garden. In 1992, after I'd returned to BC as the head coach, I went to Bird's retirement ceremony, when Magic showed up; he and Bird stood on the court in full Laker and Celtic uniforms, going down memory lane about the great games they played against each other. I brought my two youngest kids, and we sat way up in the rafters, bumping our heads on the ceiling.

Going to Fenway Park was another great experience. I loved how Yawkey Way would be shut down to car traffic, and when you approach the ballpark, you feel like you're at a carnival—*that's* how much enthusiasm people in Boston have for their Red Sox. I was at Fenway in 1991 for the commemoration of the fiftieth anniversary of Ted Williams hitting .406, and I watched from the stands as Curt Gowdy interviewed Williams on the field. If you closed your eyes and heard those two talk, and heard how vividly Williams described everything, it was like being transported back to 1941.

Speaking of history: I think sometimes about Yankee Stadium, the old one in particular. You could feel the ghosts of Ruth, Gehrig, Stengel, Berra, DiMaggio, Mantle, and all the others—to say nothing of the great New York Giants who played and coached there. My son Tim was a roommate of Brian

Cashman's when they were both young men living in New York in their early twenties, so the Yankees have always treated me and my family very well. During one game, I sat in George Steinbrenner's box next to him and Frank Robinson. Sure, I was an NFL head coach—but that doesn't mean I wasn't pinching myself talking to those two.

The same goes for the many times I talked with Reggie Jackson at the stadium. We became friendly; I really enjoyed Reggie's directness and sense of humor. Or being in the Yankee dugout with Joe Torre and then with Joe Girardi, both great managers.

I was lucky enough to throw out the first pitch at Yankee Stadium *twice*, after both our Super Bowl titles. The first time, in 2008 at the old stadium, Jorge Posada set up in front of the plate—and I waved him back to behind the plate. Then, from the rubber, I threw a strike. No matter what you've done in sports, that's pretty thrilling.

The second time, in 2012 at the new stadium, I brought four of my grandkids to the mound with me. They were young, but I wanted them to have this experience and realize how special it was. We stepped across the foul line, making sure not to touch the chalk just like major league pitchers do. Joba Chamberlain flipped the ball to me and I wound up and threw from the rubber again, this one maybe a little up and in on a righty batter, but on a good day I'd get the call. We got a nice ovation, and when it was time to leave the field, my grandkids wanted to stay out there. They couldn't stop staring up at the vastness of the stadium.

———

They say there's no better place to win than New York. I know from experience that this is true. The New York fan is very savvy and passionate. If you go to MetLife Stadium, you can feel the generations of fans who have rooted for the team since its founding in 1925. The Giants are something that has bound generations of families together; they're an institution that binds together the greatest city, or region, in the world. It's only football, sure, but it's more than football, and I was aware of that, which always gave me an extra bit of motivation.

There's a lot to be said about the New York media—some good, some not so good—but I remember clearly my first press conference as head coach of the Giants, when I looked out at a room of about one hundred people. *That* shows the importance of the Giants to the people of this area. I wanted to do my best for those people.

The Giants, the NFL's flagship franchise. The uniforms: Red, white, and blue, like America. The

Giants represent the greatest city in the greatest country in the world.

For most of my time with the Giants, we lived in Park Ridge, New Jersey, in the Bears Nest community of Tudor-style town houses where Richard Nixon had once lived. We loved it there: Our place had a nice finished basement where my office was, and the development was quiet and wooded. There were some scenic, elevated cul-de-sacs for running, and a large pool and a workout room. The food in North Jersey is incredible, of course, and there were several Italian places and a Greek place we used to go to within about fifteen minutes of us. My wife, Judy, was much more into the city than I was—she loved Broadway, and the restaurants—but I'd go to the theater with her, and during one of the multiple times we saw *Hamilton*, we went backstage because the actor who played George Washington, Christopher Jackson, was a huge Giants fan and wanted to meet us.

The best part about Jersey? The people—abrupt as they were. They didn't mince words and told you exactly what they thought, and even though I was a small-town upstate guy with a different accent, that directness suited me just fine.

My first exposure to them came when I was with the ultimate Jersey guy, Bill Parcells. It was at my first training camp as a Giants assistant in 1988 at Fairleigh Dickinson University in Madison, New Jersey. Parcells saw me doing some preparation for practice at 6 a.m. and invited me to run to the deli with him for coffee and a bagel. I said I had too much work on my plate; he said something to the effect of, *Come on, we'll be back in twenty minutes*, so we hopped in his car. When we walked into the deli, Parcells immediately started ribbing the guys behind the counter, and they went right back at him—just rapid-fire wit, back and forth. Later, when *Seinfeld* became popular, I'd think of Parcells in that deli.

The pace of the New York area hits me every time I go back. People talk faster. They formulate opinions quicker. They go harder.

My first go-around with the Giants, I'd see the Twin Towers every morning on my drive to the stadium; I remember having a picture of Judy with her friends in the city, with the Twin Towers behind her. It made me feel like we had *arrived*, in New York, that we were a part of this city. When I came back as head coach in 2004, the towers were gone, and you could feel that loss.

By Super Bowl XLII, Wellington Mara and Bob Tisch had both passed away, and you could feel their loss as well. Every Friday, Mr. Tisch would bring a sandwich into my office and sit across from me, and it was always the same message: *What can I do? How can I help?*

An early memory of Mr. Mara that sticks with me is of a time when I was an assistant in 1988. In our last game of the season, we lost a disappointing game to the Jets that knocked us out of the playoffs. The next day, when the coaches were looking at the film figuring out what went wrong, Mr. Mara came in and shook all of our hands, and thanked us for our effort.

Another image pops into my mind when I think of Mr. Mara. I'm now the Giants' head coach. It's a Monday after a loss, and we're out on the Giants Stadium field making corrections. Mr. Mara is walking laps around the field, his daily walk, and you can feel his presence and support. Then on Sunday, in the moments before the game, he's in the locker room with the team. He's telling the players: *This is my coach, and I stand behind him.*

———

Other great Giants: the people behind the scenes, who those on the outside don't think about too much but who make the organization run. Without them, we're not eleven minutes and ten seconds away from a championship.

Pat Hanlon, the vice president of communications. Pat was *my guy*—just like he was for all the Giants coaches since he started with the franchise in 1993. He's a salt-of-the-earth fellow who always had a smile on his face but had a sharp tongue that told you the way he felt. Specifically, he always told me which reporters were good people and which were assholes (his word!). He was a rock to me, someone I could talk to about anything. He still is.

Ronnie Barnes, the head trainer for the Giants. He has been with the organization since 1976, and his current title is senior vice president of medical services. If there's a more savvy, multitalented person who can maneuver in more situations than Ronnie, I've never met that person. He had the trust of the players. He had the trust of the coaches. Ann Mara called Ronnie her twelfth child, and when Mr. Mara was dying of cancer in 2005, Ronnie sat nightly vigil by his hospital bed.

Ronnie's a smart businessman who has been very successful launching a line of physical therapy clinics with Dr. Russell Warren. Heck, I've even seen him analyze construction blueprints—the guy's incredible. Even now, if there's a medical issue with me or my family, the first person I call is Ronnie. In this way, I'm like countless other people who have played or worked for the Giants.

Then there's the trio that I call my Upstairs

Team—the people I would have been helpless without.

Kim Kolbe, my assistant, and the assistant to many Giants coaches before me. (She was hired by Ray Perkins, who coached the Giants starting in 1979.) Kim was extremely competent, loyal, and to the point, an extremely smart person who didn't suffer fools. She had a lot of work to do and had no time to mince words, so if she didn't like you, she'd tell you in no uncertain terms. Fortunately, she liked me and my family.

Chris Pridy, who did all of my scheduling. Football is a game that relies heavily on scheduling and logistics, and all of that must be communicated to a large roster and coaching staff, and that was Chris's job. If a storm came and we needed to move practice inside at the last minute, for instance, that was Chris. People tend to take this stuff for granted, but it's a very important job, and Chris was an ace.

Chris was also a great "eyes and ears" guy for me—he listened to the radio on his long drives to East Rutherford from his Jersey Shore home and would keep me apprised of stuff happening around the league. He was also a voracious reader who helped me brainstorm themes and inspirational quotes for my Saturday night speeches to the team. He's a very smart guy, and I always enjoyed bouncing ideas off him.

Ed Triggs was my video guy. During my speeches to the team on Saturday nights, Ed would put together a video segment to inspire the guys. One, on the eve of Super Bowl XLII, featured that Green Day song with the emotional "time of your life" refrain. Another came before the 2011 season, and featured a girls' cross-country runner who collapsed in exhaustion before crawling her way to the finish line, winning the championship for her team. The lesson? *Finish*. The year before, when several late-season losses knocked us out of the playoffs, we didn't finish. In 2011, we did.

Back in '07, Ed was as young as most of the players, so he had a finger on the pulse of the locker room, and his insights into the mood of the team were invaluable. He was extremely loyal to me, and in 2017, I had the honor of officiating the wedding of Ed and Casey Puleo, an accountant with the Giants. The venue was MetLife Stadium; they said "I do" in the middle of the field.

I can go on and on about the great people I met with the Giants. Including the cafeteria workers, who were warm and funny in a Jersey way, sometimes profane but always kind. Even now, after all these years, these people volunteer their time for Jay Fund events at MetLife Stadium. The point here is that in the fourth quarter of Super Bowl XLII, there were many, many people behind us—including the spirits of Mr. Mara and Mr. Tisch.

Winning the Super Bowl would be for every one of those people. And for the entire New York region, and all of those generations of Giants fans. As much as we wanted it for ourselves, we wanted it for them, too.

————

But we also knew that in order to win, we'd need to stop the Patriots, who, after a holding penalty on the kickoff, took possession on their 11-yard line with 10:59 remaining in the game.

On three of their previous four drives, stretching back to the second quarter, the Patriots had started at their own 11-, 10-, and 11-yard lines. I bring this up to show that we were winning the field position battle; remember that earlier in the game, our offense had first downs at the Patriots' 17-, 19-, 31-, and 45-yard lines, yet we'd come away with only three points. We weren't just *hanging around* against the undefeated Patriots—we were outplaying them. Even now, I hear some people say we were "lucky" to win the game. To these people, I ask: *Did you actually watch the game?*

If they had, they might have noticed that we

outgained New England 338 to 274. That's almost 25 percent more yards. That's significant.

I mentioned before that we hit Tom Brady seventeen times, sacking him five times. If you're dominating the line of scrimmage to that degree, and you win the game, that's not "luck."

Back to the action: We stopped the Patriots on their next possession after one first down, forcing a punt. Then, we took over at our 29-yard line, with 9:20 left. And on the second play of our drive, we had an opportunity to take control of the game.

It was a passing play where our protection broke down; Eli had multiple defenders in his face, but he spun around to avoid a sack and scrambled to his left, outside of the numbers. (He was never fast, but Eli was much more athletic than he ever got credit for.)

On that side of the field, about ten yards away along the sideline, Plaxico was working against cornerback Ellis Hobbs. Hobbs saw Eli scrambling in the open field, so he abandoned Plaxico to go make the tackle on Eli. This left Plaxico wide open—with hardly any other defender on that side of the field.

Plaxico looked back at Eli, expecting the ball to be thrown where he was standing. But Eli expected Plaxico would sprint down the sideline, so he led him with his pass, which fell out of Plaxico's reach incomplete. It was a simple miscommunication but a big missed opportunity. Had we completed that pass, Plaxico was one cut away from being off to the races for a big play—if not a touchdown.

As it was, we went three and out. We punted it to the Patriots, who this time took control at their 20-yard line. There was 7:54 on the clock. If our defense could keep holding off Tom Brady and his offense, we'd become champions.

———

It's a cliché but it's true: Football is a game of adjustments. On their eighth drive of the night, the Patriots made a key adjustment. Brady had been battered all game, so on this eighth drive, the ball would come out of his hands quickly, to receivers running short routes. All year long, the Patriots had amassed yardage in large chunks—their fifty-seven completions of twenty yards or more led the NFL. But in Super Bowl XLII, their longest completion was for nineteen yards, and now, their hope of saving their perfect season rested on their ability to move downfield methodically.

They succeeded. Brady shrugged off a night of punishment and picked us apart, completing eight of eleven passes on the drive, none of which traveled more than a few yards in the air. He worked from the shotgun on eight of the drive's twelve plays to combat the rush, making quick reads and quick throws. Our run defense had stymied the Patriots' running backs, holding them to forty-five yards on sixteen carries, so they ran the ball only once on this possession. It was a drive that showed Brady's toughness and competitive resilience—qualities he'd exhibited before and would exhibit time and again for an astonishingly long period of time. He is the best quarterback in the game's history, and no defense, no matter how great, can keep him down forever.

During the drive, Wes Welker caught three passes for twenty-eight yards; his line for the day was 11 catches on 14 targets for 103 yards. Kevin Faulk also had two catches for sixteen yards on this drive—in terms of receptions, Faulk was the Patriots' second-leading receiver on the night with seven catches on nine targets for fifty-two yards—and five of his catches went for first downs. It's not surprising that in a game defined by our ability to get pressure on Brady, their two leading receivers were best at running underneath routes. We stopped the big plays, but we couldn't stop everything.

Up to that point in the fourth quarter, we'd contained Randy Moss, thanks to the double teams we'd consistently thrown at him: Until the Patriots' final drive, he had only two catches on nine targets, for thirty-five yards. But the Patriots adjusted on this drive, finding a way to get the ball to Moss on short routes, and he came alive, catching three passes for twenty-seven yards—including a touchdown on third-and-goal from the 6-yard line that put the Patriots up 14–10.

On the play, Moss was lined up wide on the right side, and the Patriots motioned Welker over to the slot on that same side. That meant our safety Gibril Wilson, who would have otherwise double-teamed Moss, instead double-teamed Welker—which was understandable given how much Welker had hurt us and how the Patriots had attacked the short middle of the field on that drive. This left Moss one-on-one on the outside, against cornerback Corey Webster, who was lined up with outside leverage because he expected help on the inside.

Corey's first few years in the NFL were frustrating, but over the few weeks before the Super Bowl, he'd blossomed into a stalwart corner, and remained so for the rest of his career. He had good size, good body control, good awareness, and *moxie*—but it took him a while to develop that confidence. We'd drafted him in 2005, but he'd sustained a series of small injuries that slowed his progress. Corey was quiet, but he was a serious guy and a hard worker. Through his struggles, he kept plugging away, and it all came together for him in the 2007 postseason, during which he showcased his great hands by making a key interception against Tampa Bay, and then of course picking off Brett Favre's overtime pass in Green Bay that set up our game-winning field goal. In Steve Spagnuolo's defense, the corners are key, because Steve's blitz packages often left them in man coverage. If Corey hadn't developed the way he did, Steve couldn't have dialed up all of those blitzes that were so effective. The corners, the pass rush, everything in football—it's all interconnected.

But on this third-and-six play, Corey was lined up on Moss's outside shoulder, and when Moss faked a fade to the outside, Corey had to respect it, given Moss's height and leaping ability. But Moss instead ran a slant to the *inside*, causing Corey to stumble out of his backpedal when he tried to break inside with Moss—and in a rare occurrence that night, there was nobody assigned inside to double-team Moss, who was wide open in the end zone for an easy pitch-and-catch touchdown.

Our defense had held the Patriots to two trips inside the red zone all game. Unfortunately, New England came away with touchdowns both times.

Both touchdowns came after third-down conversions in which the odds were in our favor: The first touchdown followed soon after a pass interference call on third-and-ten. The second one came on a third-and-goal from the 6.

But great offenses capitalize on their opportunities,

and the 2007 Patriots were a historically great offensive team.

———

On our sideline, we were disappointed but not discouraged. Despite the touchdown, we recognized that our defense had performed heroically. Against a team that had averaged thirty-seven points per game, they gave up only fourteen. Against a team that had averaged 411.25 yards per game, they gave up just 274 yards. Against a team that had scored points on 53 percent of their offensive possessions, best in the league by nearly ten percentage points, they allowed scores on just two of their nine drives.

Allowing a late touchdown hurt, but the bottom line was that our defense had done its job and put our offense in position to win the game.

There was 2:42 on the clock. Our offense readied itself to go out onto the field. In the moments before they did, Michael Strahan addressed our offensive linemen, the guys he'd battled in practice for years.

I wasn't aware of what he said at the time, but it was captured by NFL Films cameras and has since become one of those iconic clips, part of NFL lore. It's a perfect illustration of what I always tell people about Michael: He's the greatest natural leader I've ever been around.

—17–14 is the final, okay? 17–14, fellas, Michael says to the linemen. He paces back and forth, addressing them passionately but calmly. His words are clear and confident.

—One touchdown, we are world champions, he says. *Believe it, and it* will *happen.*

The linemen look ahead at the field, nodding in rhythm with Michael's words. When I saw it later, I was reminded of that moment earlier in the game after our twelve-men-on-the-field penalty extended the Patriots drive and I'd blown a gasket. Michael had stepped in and calmed me down. He had reassured me, and now, with that same matter-of-fact confidence, he was reassuring our offensive linemen.

Because Michael believes. Our offensive linemen believe. We all believe. 17–14. It *will* happen.

Chapter Nine

THE DRIVE THAT BINDS US TOGETHER, FOREVER

Part 1: Eli Reconnects with an Old Friend

Eli Manning is a slam-dunk Hall of Famer. Two Super Bowl–winning drives against the greatest defensive coach in the history of the league. Two Super Bowl MVPs. How can he not be?

The world might not have known what he was capable of when he led our offense onto the field with 2:39 on the clock in Super Bowl XLII, down 14–10, on our 17-yard line, but over on our sideline, we had a pretty good idea. He had already displayed a knack for locking in when the stakes were highest, and here the stakes couldn't have been higher: A touchdown, we win. Anything other than that, we lose.

Eli had come a long way, but what was inside of him was evident from the beginning of his time with the Giants. Flash back to Eli's rookie year, in that loss against Baltimore I wrote about earlier, when Eli had been blitzed and battered in his fourth straight loss to start his career. When he came into my office the next day and told me that he could be the franchise quarterback of the Giants, that he *could do it*, the look on his face told me how much he believed in himself. He was near tears, because *that* was how badly he wanted the opportunity to show who he was. That day, I saw Eli's conviction and his belief in himself. And when he took the field for the final drive in Arizona, I looked in his eyes and saw the exact same thing. He knew this was his moment, and he embraced the challenge.

That's Eli Manning. If you're looking for a big-game quarterback, there's nobody in the history of the game I'd take over him.

———

All these years later, I get goose bumps thinking of this last drive. It was the epitome of everything we were as a team. *Nothing* was easy. There were several near catastrophes, and a bunch of times when most people probably counted us out. But we picked ourselves up and kept going. We scrapped for every inch, because we'd need every inch on this drive. We persevered.

A study in perseverance on that 2007 Giants team was Amani Toomer—whose eleven-yard reception on the first play of the drive gave us a first-and-ten at the Giants' 28. On the play, New England was in zone coverage, trying to keep things in front of them and therefore giving up some ground underneath. Amani ran a curl route, getting open simply by taking what the defense was giving him. Amani was good at running curls because he could get his body under control without telegraphing that he was slowing down. That's the type of subtle skill that doesn't show up on TV but makes for a good receiver, which Amani was for the Giants for a long time.

Amani had traveled a long road to get to this point. In '07, he turned thirty-three years old and was fighting back from a partially torn ACL that had ended his previous season. For most of the regular season he was still feeling his way back, but he got rolling in the playoffs, bringing with him an experience that helped our team. He and Michael Strahan were the only two remaining players from the 2000 team that went to the Super Bowl; they were the only two guys who had won playoff games in a Giants uniform prior to the 2007 season.

Amani and Eli always had a special chemistry on the field. It had been evident early on, during one of the first great moments of Eli's career, in 2005, when Eli led us to a comeback win at home against Denver and hit Amani for a touchdown on the final drive. A big reason Eli blossomed in the '07 playoffs was Amani's return to form, beginning with his seven-catch, seventy-four-yard performance in Tampa Bay, where his fourth-quarter touchdown reception put us up 24–7, icing the game.

In Dallas, Amani's improbable fifty-two-yard touchdown on the game's opening drive let everyone in the building know this game would be different from our first two meetings. On the play, he caught a short pass but made a well-timed spin move to the outside, causing two Cowboys defenders to run into each other and lose leverage. It was a crafty veteran move, and the sight of Amani streaking down the left sideline gave a huge lift to our team.

When I came to New York, Amani was wary— he was one of many guys who believed what they'd read about me. But in short order, he evolved into being a team leader. One moment between Amani and me stands out, in terms of signifying he'd bought in: It was in 2006, during our second game of the season, a hot day in Philly on which we fell behind 24–7. But in the fourth quarter, we clawed back to tie the game and then won in overtime on an

Eli deep ball to Plaxico. After the game, I saw Amani lying on the grass, flat on his back, and I walked over. He was completely exhausted but had a huge smile on his face.

—*Coach, we did it*, he told me. *We came back and did it.*

I'll never forget it. It was such a magnificent expression of what it means to pay the price, and the elation that comes with winning.

Now here we were, sixteen months later, in Super Bowl XLII. An even better victory was right in front of us.

On our next set of downs, after two incomplete passes to Plaxico, we faced a third-and-ten, and Eli looked for Amani. He was lined up on the left side of the formation and ran an option route past the first-down sticks. But Patriots linebacker Adalius Thomas got a strong power rush off that side, right in Eli's face—it was the second play in a row Thomas had done so—which prevented Eli from stepping into his throw.

Consequently, the ball came low and outside to Amani, but Amani lunged forward and caught it while falling to the ground. It was a great catch, but in order for him to secure the ball, he landed short of the first-down marker, bringing up fourth down and a half yard to go.

That catch closed out Amani's game on the stat

sheet: He was our leading receiver, catching six passes on six targets for eighty-four yards. Amani has said that the Giants' 34–7 loss to the Baltimore Ravens in Super Bowl XXXV still haunts him, because, he says, the Giants "didn't give our best shot." In Super Bowl XLII, nobody could ever say Amani Toomer didn't give it his best shot.

He'd given us the opportunity to extend our drive. But now, with 1:34 remaining, needing about eighteen inches, our season would come down to the next play.

Part 2: Survivors

Years later, while watching the Fox broadcast of the game, I noticed that Troy Aikman questioned whether or not we'd go for it on fourth down.

In today's game, with the way decision-making has evolved, this wouldn't be a question. Frankly, it wasn't a question in my mind at the time: There was no way I was giving the ball back to Tom Brady, who would've needed just one first down to clinch the game. I had faith in our offense's ability to move the ball a half yard.

As far as the play call: We felt that with the season on the line, we needed to go with our best, the thing that got us to this point in the first place. The foundation of our offense was our power-running game, and the foundation of our running game was the right side of our line. We knew that, and we knew the Patriots knew that.

So, no surprises. We ran an off-tackle slam to Brandon Jacobs, our 265-pound back, behind our two strongest men: Chris Snee and Kareem McKenzie, with the play designed to go between the two of them. Fullback Madison Hedgecock would provide a lead block.

The Patriots got good penetration, however, and the point of attack was heavily trafficked with bodies. In particular, linebacker Tedy Bruschi got into our backfield, so Hedgecock had to block him, which meant Brandon didn't have much room to maneuver or generate forward momentum.

But Brandon would not be denied. He wiggled and willed his way forward. He lunged, and then, while falling to the ground, stretched out his arm carrying the ball about six inches past the first-down marker.

Our faith in our team's physicality was rewarded. It wasn't pretty and it wasn't clean, but then again, the 2007 Giants weren't known for being pretty or clean. The thing we had going for us was a tremendous will to survive. By the skin of our teeth, we had survived again.

We survived the two subsequent plays as well, again by thin margins.

On our ensuing first-and-ten, Adalius Thomas beat David Diehl around the edge with a hesitation move on a speed rush and flushed Eli out of the pocket. Eli scrambled five yards downfield, but Thomas caught him from behind, and while Eli was being dragged to the ground, he briefly fumbled the ball before immediately falling on top of it. It was a near miss and a scary moment.

On the subsequent play, a second-and-five, Eli looked for David Tyree, who was lined up wide on the right side. But the two had a miscommunication on the route, and when Eli tried to throw the ball away out of bounds, he didn't get quite enough zip on the ball—giving Patriots cornerback Asante Samuel an opportunity to intercept the ball along the sideline.

Watching the play, you can tell Samuel was a little surprised the ball was thrown his way. Because of that, he didn't fully load for his jump, and the pass grazed off the fingertips of his outstretched arms because he didn't quite get high enough to catch it cleanly. Some people have characterized this as a missed interception, but I disagree with that: I'd say the ball was *just* out of his reach.

There were several such plays on the drive— where the Patriots, maybe, could have made a play that ended our season. But they didn't.

That's sports. It sounds so simple to say, but the team that makes those plays wins, and the team that doesn't loses. The Patriots didn't make that play. But now, with a third-and-five from our 44-yard line, with 1:15 left in the game, having survived two scares, we needed to make one.

Part 3: The Helmet Catch

David Tyree was a survivor.

Nearly four years before his most famous moment, David found himself in my office. I was the newly installed head coach of the Giants, and David had screwed up. Police in Fort Lee, New Jersey, had pulled him over for speeding and discovered a half pound of marijuana in his car.

He'd been teetering on the edge for years. An ace special teamer and a blue-collar player on the field, David couldn't resist the pull of the streets off the field. Alcohol and marijuana were a regular part of his life since he was a kid. He once told the *New York Times* that former Giants coach Jim Fassel fined him $10,000 for being late to a team meeting. He thanked Coach Fassel for setting him straight—then hit the streets to sell drugs so he could recoup the fine.

A few days after his arrest, Ernie Accorsi called him into the facility and told him to go to my office. It was my call, Ernie told me, whether to keep him or cut him.

My office was David's last stop before unemployment—and the last place he wanted to be. My reputation for not tolerating bad behavior preceded me. In my first weeks as the Giants' coach, I was trying to establish the foundation of a team composed of guys who demonstrated good character, on and off the field.

Think about the stakes for David here: He was a kid from North Jersey who went to Syracuse like I did, and who'd worked his whole life to play for his hometown team. But in my office, he was on the edge of a cliff, with just his toes keeping him from falling off. During that meeting, he had about five minutes to convince me of why I should keep him.

As for me, I would mostly stay silent. I wanted to see what David would say for himself.

What he did was break down in tears, asking for another chance. He owned up to everything he'd done, but said he'd changed. He said he had become religious and had dedicated himself to God. He was going to be a much better man and a much better teammate.

I'd seen this same sort of thing from other players in the past—it's human nature to beg for one more chance. But in David's case, this particular time, my intuition told me he was sincere. I can't explain it any more than that: It was a hunch. Something in David's demeanor told me he'd found the clarity

220

that comes with almost losing it all. That despite his mistakes, he was fundamentally a good young man.

When David walked out of my office that day, he was still a New York Giant.

———

Fast-forward some three and a half years. It was a Saturday night in December 2007, and we were staying at a hotel in Jersey before a home game against Washington.

Since his arrest in 2004, David had made good on his word. He had married his then girlfriend and become a dedicated father, as well as a beloved teammate. A charismatic guy, he had great skill in weaving his spiritual beliefs into messages about pride, team, and sacrifice. But he didn't overdo it in that regard—mostly, he brought his lunch pail and let his work speak for itself. There hadn't been one moment that I regretted my decision to give him another chance, something that remains true: David was the Giants' director of player development from 2014 to 2017—and on a personal note, he has always been willing to help out with Jay Fund events.

As a player, he was probably the best special teams guy in the league, making the Pro Bowl in 2005. He had good enough speed, but more important, he was strong and fearless, with a willingness to fly around at high speeds and stick his nose in harm's way to make tackles. He played on all the special teams: kickoff, kick return, punt return, and the punt team, where he made his biggest contribution as our gunner. When I watched David work with Jeff Feagles, the league's premier directional punter, it was almost like watching a quarterback throwing a fade to a receiver.

It had been a long time since that fateful day in my office, but on this Saturday night before the Washington game, David was in tears again. We were in our evening meeting when the organization got the horrible news: David's mother had just died at age fifty-nine. David was pulled from the meeting and given the news by his wife. He and his mother were extremely close; they'd become born-again Christians together a few years before, and together the two of them had turned their lives around.

I got out of the meeting and saw David sitting by the hotel elevators, sobbing uncontrollably. His teammates were trying to console him, and I walked over to him and tried to do the same. But of course words don't mean much at a time like that.

After his mom's death, as an organization, we told him to take however long he needed to process his loss. He wound up missing the Washington game and our game the following week at Buffalo.

During that week, there was a wake in New Jersey, and I attended along with John Mara, general manager Jerry Reese, and most of the players.

We were there for him. We all had tremendous respect for the person he'd become. And that would've been the case regardless of what happened with 1:15 remaining in Super Bowl XLII, on a third-and-five from our 44-yard line.

———

The play was called 62 Y Sail Union. David was split wide on the right side, one of four receivers. He was supposed to run a post. Steve Smith, in the slot position on David's side, would run a corner route. On the other side, Plaxico Burress and Amani Toomer would run in-breaking routes.

But within instants of the snap, it was obvious Eli wouldn't have time to get the ball to anyone. The Patriots beat us so badly on the snap of the ball that Eli was fighting for his life by the time the receivers got into their breaks.

Two Patriots got a grip on Eli: Richard Seymour, a Hall of Famer who was about one hundred pounds bigger than Eli, and Jarvis Green, who outweighed Eli by about seventy pounds. But Eli, with the help of some of our linemen who didn't quit on the play, fought through the tackle attempts to twist himself loose. When considering Eli's legacy, know this: A lesser competitor would've gone down.

After freeing himself, Eli's momentum carried him to his right, where he darted to an open patch of field. Forty-three yards away, at the Patriots' 24-yard line, was David, who knew Eli was in distress and was working his way back to the quarterback, which all receivers are trained to do.

Eli spotted a white flash downfield wearing number 85. David was open.

Recall our Friday practice before the game, when David was dropping every pass thrown to him. Eli had told him to shake it off, to not worry about it, because he knew David would be there for us when it counted. By that point, David Tyree had earned everyone's trust.

Eli gathered himself and heaved the ball toward the middle of the field, to David.

———

People call it a "lucky" catch, and that bothers me. It diminishes our team's accomplishment, as if "the Helmet Catch" is shorthand for "a lucky win." In reality, we outplayed the Patriots that day. The stats don't lie.

The characterization also diminishes David's

accomplishment. Watch the play closely: David trapped the ball against his helmet, yes, but that was only *after* he reeled it in cleanly with both hands above his head—only for Rodney Harrison to swat at the ball and knock David's left hand off it. After that, David momentarily pinned the ball with his *right* hand against his helmet, before securing it again with *both* hands as he fell to the ground. It's a credit to David, and his strong hands, that he found a way to hold on to the ball after an All-Pro safety made a great effort to jar it loose.

But to me, the most impressive aspect of the play was this: As David was falling backward, Harrison pulled him down and slid his own body across the crooks of David's knees. That's an extremely awkward, vulnerable position for anyone to be in, and the instinctive tendency is to let go of everything to protect your knees. But David's competitive reflex won out. He didn't take his hands off the ball; his focus remained securing it with both hands, which he ultimately did. In that moment, the biggest in his career, catching the ball was more important for David than saving his knees.

Was that luck? No way. It was competitive greatness.

That's who David Tyree is. That's the type of man and teammate he assured me he was becoming several years prior, in my office, when he tearfully pleaded with me to keep him on the Giants. He'd proven it countless times before that moment in the Super Bowl. He'd just proven it again, in the process setting us up to finish the greatest upset in NFL history.

Part 4: The Most Overlooked Play of the Game

In the highlight films, it's made to seem that after David's catch, us scoring a touchdown was a formality. In real life, we still had a lot of work to do.

There would be more heart-attack moments. It wouldn't have been the 2007 Giants otherwise.

The first thing we did after David's catch was to call time-out, our second, to stop the clock and not waste the time it would take for our offense to get downfield. But on the first play after the time-out, Adalius Thomas used an inside power move to sack Eli.

Thomas, an athletic specimen with rare quickness and size, was a nightmare for us on the drive—in addition to his forced fumble on Eli a few plays earlier, he had been one of the Patriots defenders who'd broken through on the Helmet Catch play. His effectiveness owed to the simple fact that everyone in the building knew we were going to pass, allowing Thomas to showcase his full arsenal of pass rush moves. On the next play, Thomas got to Eli again on a power rush, causing an errant throw that Patriots safety Brandon Meriweather *almost* intercepted when the ball went off his fingertips.

So it was with this epic last drive: Mere eyelashes separated the heroic plays from the missed opportunities.

This brought up third-and-eleven, from the Patriots' 25, setting the stage for the most overlooked play of the game. It's fitting that it came from Steve Smith, who himself was always overlooked because of his modest size and the fact that he didn't have blazing speed.

The play was 62 Cafe X Glance—it was actually the second straight time we called that play. Steve, who was on the three-receiver side, aligned two yards outside the right tackle, ran a flat route. We had three receivers lined up on that right side, and moments after the snap, amid all that traffic, Meriweather collided with Amani Toomer, who was lined up outside of Steve in the right slot. This slowed Meriweather down and left Steve wide open in the right flat, while Meriweather sprinted to catch up.

Eli spotted Steve, but throwing to him presented a gamble: Steve's route took him near the sideline, and he was well short of the first-down marker— and Meriweather was closing fast. But Eli's instincts took over and he threw to Steve without hesitation. For his part, Steve, being the smart, intuitive athlete he is, turned his body while the ball was coming in, positioning himself to dart upfield. He hauled in the pass, then shuffled past the first-down marker before Meriweather knocked him out of bounds.

Steve Smith, a rookie, had made a savvy, veteran play in the most important of moments. It was representative of a season in which the rookies had played beyond their years.

Now it was first-and-ten from the Patriots' 13-yard line, with the clock stopped at 0:39. It was time to win the game.

Part 5: Finish the Job

Our offensive coordinator, Kevin Gilbride, never got enough credit. All you need to know about Kevin is this: There are four Lombardi Trophies at the team headquarters at 1925 Giants Drive in East Rutherford, and Kevin called every offensive play for two of them.

Kevin and I go back to Jacksonville in the 1990s, when I was the Jaguars' first head coach and he was our offensive coordinator. His career shows that the most important quality for a coach is adaptability: He'd been successful earlier in the '90s with the

Houston Oilers, when his run-and-shoot offense finished in the NFL's top three in yards for four straight years. Then, he went to Jacksonville and made two AFC Championship games with a run- and play-action-based system. Now he was in New York calling plays in a Super Bowl with that same type of offense.

Sometimes, being adaptable means changing your philosophy to bring out the best in your personnel. Sometimes, being adaptable means doing something you've never done before, if the situation calls for it. After Steve's first down, Kevin liked what he saw with our route combination against the Patriots' defense. So he called the same play from the same formation again—for the *third* straight time. He has said it was the only time in his career that he'd done that.

Like so many of Kevin's calls, it was the right play for the right moment.

———

The play called for Plaxico to line up wide on the left, the sole receiver on that side with three receivers on the right side. He was tasked with running a fade. As our offense broke the huddle, Eli told Plax that if he was single covered, the ball was coming to him.

But Plax didn't think the Patriots would cover him one-on-one. All game long, on about 75 percent of our passing plays, he'd been double-teamed. He'd gutted through the knee injury he'd sustained earlier in the week, and even though he didn't have a great stat line—two catches on nine targets for twenty-seven yards—the attention he received from the defense shows how important his determined effort was.

When Plax lined up, he saw the Patriots' defenders showing blitz, with cornerback Ellis Hobbs in single coverage against him, and his eyes lit up. He had prepared for this moment: An avid student of the game, Plax had noticed on film that when Hobbs was defending inside the 10-yard line and went into a backpedal, he tended to stop his backpedal around the goal line. From seeing that, Plax knew that if he faked a slant before breaking into the fade, he'd have Hobbs beat easily.

But there was a problem: Selling the slant would require Plax to push hard off his left knee—his injured knee. In the years since that play, he has said that he didn't know whether his knee would even hold up. But Plax is a competitor, and this was the Super Bowl. Before the play, he decided to throw caution to the wind.

There's a Confucius quote that encapsulates my philosophy of coaching. If you'd indulge me and my master's degree in secondary education, it's really my philosophy of *teaching*: "I hear and I forget. I see and I remember. I do and I understand."

Every day in practice, as coaches, we're trying to instill a comprehensive understanding among our players. We talk to them, but that only goes so far. We show them film, and that helps a little bit more. Then we get out on the practice field and put it into action, again and again and again, and that's where the learning clicks into place.

On offense, we practiced going against blitzes thousands of times. As a coach, it's something I place the highest priority on. When Eli Manning was a rookie, before he became our starter, I gave him a notebook and told him to spend however long it took to diagram every blitz the opponent had run all year, and how he would protect against it. Running backs who play for me must first prove they can pick up the blitz—they can be all-world as a runner, but if they don't understand protection schemes and don't have the physicality to block a blitzing linebacker, they don't play on my team. As a former wide receivers coach, recognizing a blitz and the "hot" route response to it is a constant point of emphasis.

In football games, blitzes are when the money's

on the line. They're either really good for the defense or really good for the offense. If your players don't know exactly how to react, you're in trouble. If they do, the opponent's in trouble.

With thirty-nine seconds left in Super Bowl XLII, when the Patriots came with an all-out blitz, we knew how to react.

The free rusher, safety Rodney Harrison, came off the offensive right side; Brandon Jacobs, the running back on the play who was lined up on the *left* side, didn't hesitate and went across the formation to put a textbook block on him. This meant Eli had time and space to throw the ball.

Eli had already prepared for the blitz before the snap; that was what his conversation with Plax was all about. After he recognized the blitz, he released the ball quickly, high into the back-left corner of the end zone. This gave Plax time to locate the ball and run underneath it.

Meanwhile, on the sideline, I saw the ball, and I saw Plax wide open. The ball hung in the air long enough that I remember thinking: *Is this ball ever gonna come down?*

The ball began its descent. My next thought was, *Just catch the ball, Plax.*

In theory, it was the easiest catch imaginable. But sometimes there's *too* much time, so that it throws off your athletic rhythm—like when a basketball player has an open shot, and there's nobody even close to him. You can get mesmerized by the ball in the air; you can start to think about things that are usually second nature.

Plax turned toward the ball and used his hands to secure it against his chest.

Touchdown, Giants.

The crowd went crazy. Our sideline went crazy.

I have a vivid mental image of Plax from after the game. He's going into the interview room, holding his young son and with his wife beside him, and he's in tears. Plax could be distant and hard for me to reach, but everything about his 2007 season showed just how much he cared. All year long, he'd played through with a damaged ankle tendon. In this game, he played despite being on one leg, and his presence itself was a big reason we gained 338 yards that day against a defense that gave up 288 yards per game during the regular season, good for 17 percent more.

I can picture Plax in meetings during his time with the Giants: He's sitting with a partition partially shielding him, because he doesn't want me to see his eyes. Sometimes, he was aloof and didn't want us to know he cared. But he did. Our receivers coach, Mike Sullivan, would routinely see Plax alone on Fridays watching extra film, long after his fellow receivers had left. It was that film study that led to his go-ahead touchdown in the Super Bowl.

Of course, at the time, I'm not thinking about any of this. I'm thinking about the time on the clock— now 0:39—and about stopping the Patriots. In fact, the Fox cameras captured me screaming at the offensive players to get back on the sideline so we could line up for the extra point.

Thirty-nine seconds meant it wasn't time to celebrate. We still had to be in battle mode. If there's anything the modern NFL has taught us, it's that great quarterbacks can lead their team downfield in shockingly little time. And Tom Brady was the best quarterback of them all.

Part 6: Bring on the Confetti

The Patriots took over at their own 26-yard line; they now had twenty-nine seconds. In order to get to our, say, 30-yard line, which would allow them a seemingly makeable forty-eight-yard field goal, they needed forty-four yards. They had three time-outs. This game was far from over.

On their first play, Spagnuolo dialed up a max blitz, bringing defensive backs Gibril Wilson and Kevin Dockery off the defensive right side.

About a year before, when I'd interviewed Steve for the defensive coordinator job, I was impressed with his aggressive mindset and his belief that the defense should dictate terms to the offense. Calling a max blitz in this situation was certainly consistent with this mindset. The blitz caused Brady to rush his throw, and Aaron Ross almost intercepted the pass before it fell incomplete.

On the next play, our rookie nose tackle, Jay Alford, beat his man with a quick inside move and charged at Brady. He drilled Brady in the ribs, putting him on his back for a sack and a ten-yard loss. It was our fifth sack of the night and an exclamation point on a game where our pass rushers, going against the best offense in the history of the sport, consistently outplayed the men across from them.

On their third-down play, the Patriots, not wanting to subject Brady to our pass rushers anymore, rolled him out to the right side. This time, he had space to step into his throw, which hadn't been the case most of the night, and he launched a missile sixty-five yards downfield toward Randy Moss, who was running down our left sideline. But Corey Webster stayed with Moss and deflected the pass away, another in a long line of great plays he made that postseason.

On fourth-and-twenty, with ten seconds left on the clock, down to their last chance, the Patriots tried that matchup again: The greatest quarterback who ever played threw the ball seventy yards in the air to the Hall of Fame receiver streaking down the sideline. But we had two people, Corey and Gibril, in position, and Gibril broke up the pass.

After the turnover on downs, one second remained on the clock. Our offense proudly jogged onto the field one last time in the 2007 season. It was time for victory formation—my favorite formation.

We had just pulled off the biggest upset in Super Bowl history.

Chapter Ten

CANYON OF HEROES

The moments afterward are kind of a blur—starting with the Gatorade dunk, a tradition that began the year the Giants won their first Super Bowl, under Bill Parcells. The confetti rains down, you raise the Lombardi Trophy at a midfield podium, and for the next few hours, it's like you're in a dream world, being taken from one place to the next, one media appearance after another, carried along by your happiness. It took forever to get to the locker room; I never actually got the opportunity to give that one speech to all the guys where I could say, *We are world champions.*

Some images stick out to me: Amid the chaos on the field, finding Judy and my family and embracing them. Seeing my then-four-year-old granddaughter,

Emma, in my son Tim's arms—she said to me, *Pop-Pop, did the Giants win?* Watching Emma and my grandson Dylan, who was also four, both wearing Chris Snee jerseys, making snow angels with confetti in the end zone. Then, in the locker room, witnessing Peyton and Eli talking to each other. It was an emotional, intense scene, with Peyton doing most of the talking.

It was about 12:30 in the morning before I could even take a shower. Judy had organized a small party with friends and family in my hotel suite. I couldn't help thinking that sixteen hours before, I was making my final preparations while my grand-kids crawled all over me—and doodled all over my notes and game plans. Now I was back in that suite, grateful for so many things in my life. Downstairs, in the hotel lobby, the Giants had a big party for all the players, staff, and families, and I walked around for a bit but didn't stay for long. In just a few hours, we'd be on a bus heading to the airport for a cross-country flight.

I slept about three hours. The first person I saw in the morning when I left my suite was Tim, in the hotel hallway. He told me he'd stayed up all night, watching the game over and over to make sure it had really happened.

I headed off to the morning press conference. While looking out at the packed media room, it occurred to me that none of those reporters and writers had picked the Giants to win this game. I also thought about a previous media appearance, a day or two before the game, when the person I followed on the podium was Don Shula—coach of the 1972 Miami Dolphins, whose perfect season, everyone thought, would be topped by New England. When we saw each other that day, Coach Shula said to me, *Good luck, Tom.*

After the press conference, we flew home to Jersey. The mood on the flight was tired but happy.

The following day, Tuesday, was the parade along the Canyon of Heroes in Lower Manhattan. I had mixed feelings about it before it happened: I'd seen the clips of Eisenhower and Truman going down Broadway after World War II, and I told John Mara it didn't quite feel right to get the same treatment. But getting out there blew my mind. It was incredible, truly a bucket list experience. Two million people packed into a few blocks downtown, spilling out of everywhere—on the streets, the side streets, sticking their heads out of buildings. Going down Broadway had all the magnificent power of a great canyon in nature, except the people were the scenery.

It was a warm January day, with temperatures in the fifties, so our guys were comfortable as they soaked it all in. We felt all of the power and magnitude of New York City. We felt the love that New York has for its Giants.

One image that sticks out to me was when we passed by Trinity Church, the historic church at Broadway and Wall Street. The rector, Jim Cooper, is a friend of mine whom I'd known from Jacksonville. When our float passed by, he was standing on a ladder, in full vestments but wearing a Giants Super Bowl hat, waving incense to bless the Super Bowl champions as we passed by. I thought to myself: *Only in New York*.

At City Hall, Michael Strahan spoke at the podium and showcased his natural charisma. When he did his *Stomp you out!* routine, the crowd went wild.

After that, we got on buses to East Rutherford for a reception at the stadium for our Jersey-based fans—the Giants' fan base is too big for just one celebration. We were joined on the stage at midfield by Chris Christie, then the governor of New Jersey and a huge Cowboys fan. Christie didn't take the microphone, gritting his teeth and refusing to crack a smile the whole time, but he knew he could benefit politically from being onstage with us. But the fans didn't come to see the politicians. They came to see us, and they went berserk when David Tyree re-enacted his instantly famous Helmet Catch, grabbing a football and holding it to his head.

It was a great day, and I soaked it in as best I could. But that's really not a strength of mine. I've always been a *What's next?* kind of guy, pointed forward toward the next challenge, a little too aware of the work that needs to be done to fully enjoy the moment. It's both a blessing and a curse: Everything I've achieved, it's because I'm this way. But sometimes I wish I could've slowed things down and enjoyed things a bit more, like I imagine how someone wired differently would. I wish I had shared all the emotions I was feeling with my family a little bit more. I wish I could put those feelings in a bottle, where, when I'm feeling nostalgic, I could just pop a cork and transport myself back to that moment. But life doesn't work that way. Everything is always moving forward, and so am I. In the NFL especially, change happens quickly, and you don't get back to the top of the mountain by standing still.

There's a picture of me taken shortly after Super Bowl XLII that I've always felt captures me perfectly. I'm sitting at my desk with my feet up and a contented expression on my face. In the foreground, on my desk, is the Vince Lombardi Trophy. Behind me is a dry-erase board, with the words "MISSION ACCOMPLISHED!" written on it. But in my hand is a clicker. I'm watching game film.

When one mission is accomplished, the next one is beginning. The work doesn't stop. Life goes on.

To that point: After going down the Canyon of Heroes, after the reception at Giants Stadium, after all the speeches, what did I do next?

Well, months prior, I'd scheduled a dentist appointment for that day. So after a day of adulation, Tom Coughlin, newly minted Super Bowl–winning coach, went to the dentist and got his teeth cleaned.

———

Almost three months later, on April 30, long after everyone had scattered for the off-season, we met up again near where our championship run began: Washington, DC. About seven months prior, we'd been 0-2 before Greg Gadson came to our hotel and inspired our team, helping to turn our season around. Now, we were set to visit Walter Reed Army Medical Center before going to the White House.

At Walter Reed, we reconnected with Greg, seeing him for the first time since the Super Bowl. He'd been in his wheelchair during the game, but he'd be joining us at the White House; he was determined to stand on prosthetic legs, and he'd been working tirelessly to do so. Greg and I embraced and caught up, and at a certain point he said, *So when are you guys moving on to next year?* and I laughed. I liked his attitude, because that's my attitude as well.

Our focus during the visit was the Military Advanced Training Center, where soldiers who have lost limbs go for rehabilitation. Being in their presence was emotional and humbling: I was in awe of their courage, sacrifice, and positive attitude. One soldier sitting in a wheelchair with only one leg congratulated me on the Super Bowl, and then thanked us for visiting. But I told him, *You're the hero. We're here to thank you.*

After Walter Reed, we took a bus to 1600 Pennsylvania Avenue, which was an experience of a lifetime. Before the ceremony, we got a tour of the White House, and then President George W. Bush emerged to greet a small group of us that included Eli and Amani. A former owner of the Texas Rangers baseball team, President Bush is a big sports fan, and he impressed us with his knowledge as we talked about the game.

When it was finally time to go to the South Lawn for the ceremony, President Bush gave a speech about our team, highlighting our Week 17 game against the Patriots: *Your team didn't win on the scoreboard, but you won the hearts of a lot of Americans for contesting the game,* he said.

Then it was my turn to speak; I stepped to the podium with President Bush a few feet to the side of me. I mentioned that people called us the "Road Warriors"—but that we paled in comparison to the true warriors we'd just seen at Walter Reed. Then we presented the president with a couple of gifts, including a ball signed by the entire team, and I told him:

When you place this championship ball in your trophy case, and you pass by the ball, we would ask hopefully that you would reflect on the accomplishments of this great group of young men. A group of men who believed in themselves, who refused to be beaten, and brought great honor and glory to the great game of professional football.

At a certain point during my speech, the realization hit me: Here I am, a guy from Church Street in Waterloo, New York, standing next to the president of the United States. Football had brought me a long way.

I had that same thought the following month when our team went to Tiffany in Manhattan for a presentation of our Super Bowl rings. Michael Strahan had always joked that he wanted a "ten-table ring"—that is, a ring that can be seen by someone who's sitting ten tables away at a restaurant—and this one fit the bill. It was magnificent, with its diamond-studded face showing the three Vince Lombardi trophies the Giants had won to that point. Personally, I was impressed with how much information they got on that ring, including your name and the score of the Super Bowl.

I don't wear mine often, but I do break it out for special occasions, like when I visit children at a hospital—the kids and their families always love seeing it and putting it on. It's great for that reason, and also as a physical reminder that for one year, we were world champions. All the 2007 Giants have that ring, and the knowledge that we do binds us together for the rest of our lives.

A few weeks later, on July 12, I went back to Waterloo, where the town held a parade in my honor. It was a warm, sunny day, a few months and two million people removed from the Canyon of Heroes. We walked through the streets of my youth, and when I saw some of the guys from my high school football team, the memories of those two championships came pouring back.

In the years since Super Bowl XLII, Waterloo High School has named its stadium after me, and the town's "Welcome" sign now mentions that it's my hometown as well as the birthplace of Memorial Day. I'm deeply honored, as I was at the parade when they unveiled a mural featuring pictures of me throughout the years, from my high school teams to the Super Bowl.

The mural refers to me as a "humble hero"— someone who "continues to make his dreams into reality." This means everything to me. Because Waterloo was where I dreamed. It was where I played pickup football on the library and church lawns and let my imagination take over: *I'm Jim Brown. I'm Ernie Davis.*

It all started with dreams. Then came a lot of hard work. Decades later, here I was, back in Waterloo, having become what I'd always dreamed of becoming: a Super Bowl champion.

———

JUDY

There's a photo from Super Bowl XLII that's very special to me: Moments after the final gun, in the stands, my wife, Judy, and some of our children and grandchildren are pictured. Judy's expression is worth a million words—it's pure joy. With everything she has sacrificed through the decades, winning the Super Bowl is the culmination of her journey as well as mine. She has always been a champion, but in this moment, in the prime of her life and surrounded by the people she loves, she has been crowned.

Years ago, growing up as a young kid in Waterloo, I knew who Judy Whitaker was, but I didn't know her personally. At Waterloo High School, where she was in the grade above me, she was very popular. She was a cheerleader with an effervescent personality. Her smile could light up the room, and when she talked to someone, she treated them like the most important person in the world. Needless to say, she seemed completely out of my league.

We went out for the first time because my best friend started dating Judy's best friend; I was a junior and she was a senior. I was an athlete and so was she, a gifted and graceful ice skater who'd swum three miles across Cayuga Lake at age twelve. To pass the time, sometimes we'd play catch with a football or maybe shoot baskets. She came from a great family—her dad was an entrepreneur and developer, her mom a teacher—and she had the confidence that came from that foundation. Her demeanor was always calm and cool, like she was always aware of the circumstances and always in control. As everyone knows, I have a temper and can fly off the handle. Judy and I balanced each other out perfectly.

What did she see in me? Was it my movie-star looks, or maybe my famous easy charm? My best guess is my work ethic. During summers in college, I worked for her dad doing construction on some of his developments, where the guys on the job would hand me an air hammer and say, *Let the kid do it*. Anything I did, I did to the best of my ability, and I think she admired that about me. She also really liked my family—she'd come over and talk to my sisters and have a cup of coffee with my mother. Whatever it was she saw in me, I'm just grateful it worked out.

We got married just before my senior year of college. Judy had graduated from Brockport State University, a teachers college where she was studying to follow her mother into the profession. When she was at Brockport and I was at Syracuse, we were about three hours apart, so mostly we wrote letters to each other because that was what you did in those days.

When I graduated from Syracuse, I began my long climb through the coaching ranks, starting with my graduate assistant job at Syracuse. Judy had trained to become a teacher, and for two years, she taught phys ed and coached track at a high school in Syracuse. But soon after, she embarked on a career that's equally challenging, a career that's as difficult as any career: She became a coach's wife.

Being a coach's wife means your life is being uprooted constantly. Being a coach's wife means your husband works crazy hours and isn't around nearly as much as you both want. Being a coach's wife means your husband lives with tunnel vision, focused completely on the next week's game to the exclusion of everything else.

Through the years, while I was obsessing over

this or that detail having to do with football, Judy had a great way of cutting through all that to remind me what was really important. She was always kind, but with me, she would use sarcasm to get her point across. Example: After a season in which my coach's hours took me away from home for long stretches, I'd come home and start giving orders to the kids—I couldn't help it; I'm a coach and that's in my nature. But then Judy would give me just one look, one raised eyebrow, to say what needed to be said: *Who do you think you are? I'm in charge here and I've got this covered.*

And she did. I've never met a more competent person who could handle everything in stride, with dignity and positive energy. Every real estate transaction (because we moved constantly), every home improvement or construction project—heck, every time something broke in the house—she was the person who handled it.

In every new place we moved to, Judy would quickly endear herself to the community—we still get Christmas cards from people we met at those Friday night fish fries in Green Bay, where I was an assistant in the mid-'80s. It's that quality I talked about, where she makes people feel like they're the most important in the world. That quality was on display every Sunday, where she'd hug the players after the game when they'd come out of the locker room. She would watch the games in a suite, and every Christmas, she'd give gifts to all the employees in the suite.

Judy was beloved—ask anyone who ever played for me. Ask Richie Seubert and Antonio Pierce, who both suffered career-ending injuries and say Judy's support helped get them through those tough times. When somebody needed a lift, Judy was always there.

The phrase "my better half" was meant for me and Judy, who, if you ask my players, was certainly more likable than me. Michael Strahan put it best in the NFL Films *A Football Life* documentary about me: *Thank God for Judy. If there was no Judy, there'd be no Super Bowls.*

———

The greatest gift she ever gave me is the family we share together. Four children with wonderful spouses. Twelve grandkids.

There has never been a better mother or grandmother. She was always patient, always positive. The capacity she had in her heart for love and understanding was limitless. Our kids are all unique, and she understood each of them in a profound way.

Keli was our first, born in 1969. Even when she was a child, you could tell she was a lot like her mother—someone who gets along with everyone and who makes it her business to be nice. She studied to be an athletic trainer and went to grad school at Michigan State University because the school allowed women to be trainers for the football team, and Keli was interested in identifying and rehabilitating the type of serious injuries you'd see on the gridiron.

She was a very successful trainer, progressing to become the head athletic trainer at the University of North Florida. But after I launched the Jay Fund, and the organization got big enough to demand full-time staff, she became its executive director and then its CEO. I felt I needed someone like her to run the organization—Keli combines the best qualities of Judy and me. She's a people person, whose demeanor makes it obvious that she genuinely cares about people, but at the same time she's a natural motivator who wants to lead her team. It's often been said that in her role at the Jay Fund, she's her father's daughter. This makes me immensely proud. She and her husband, Chris Joyce, live in the Jacksonville area with their two children: Marin Elizabeth and Clara Amelia.

Our second child, Tim, was born in 1972. Tim

was an outstanding athlete from the start: As a small child, whenever I'd pitch to him, I'd come back home bruised because of all the balls he'd smack right back at me. He'd later go on to play a year of football at the University of Virginia and then become a key contributor on the baseball team; he was the captain and played third base.

Tim and his wife, Andrea, live in New Jersey with their three children: Emma Rose, Shea Thomas, and Brennon Timothy. As a child, Tim was high-energy and quick-witted, one of those kids who knew all the angles and was one step ahead. It makes sense that he went into financial markets, where he has done well.

On September 11, 2001, Tim was working on the sixtieth floor of Tower 2 of the World Trade Center. I was in Jacksonville at the time and it was a Tuesday—game plan day, which meant I was in the video room with the other coaches. Keli was the first who called me: *Dad, do you know what's going on?*

I didn't, and learning what was going on was every parent's worst nightmare. After many busy signals, we finally connected with Tim on his cell phone. He said that after the first plane hit Tower 1, he and his coworkers went to the forty-fourth floor of their building for a security debriefing, as they were trained to do. There, building security told them to go back to their offices—but Tim didn't do that. Despite what the security people had said, a voice in his head told him to leave the building, so he did, and so did a number of his colleagues. My only explanation for why Tim survived was that the Holy Spirit took him by the hand and walked him out of the building.

It was a miracle that he lived, for which I'm eternally grateful. But whenever I reflect on that, I mourn the thousands who died. Tim remembers walking downstairs, past firefighters rushing past him upstairs to go into four-thousand-degree temperatures, knowing they weren't coming back. To this day, I'm moved by that, and my respect for first responders is limitless. Tim lost a lot of friends that day. A lot of people lost friends and loved ones. It was an awful, awful day and I think about it often. It's a reminder of the sacrifices so many have made to protect our freedom, and about the fragility of life. Tomorrow isn't promised to anyone.

Brian, our third child, was born in 1977. When he was born, I looked at Judy and said, *This little guy's gonna do a lot of stuff with me. This guy's gonna be my pal.* And he was. As a kid, he'd be on the sidelines during BC football games, where he'd hold the headset of one of the coaches and hear language from me he wasn't used to hearing at home.

From the time he was a little boy, Brian has always had an ability to express himself and get along with people much older, with a maturity beyond his years. Once, when he was about four or five, I remember reprimanding him for something. He looked up at me, and with an adult expression and demeanor, said, *Dad, that's not fair.* It makes sense that he wound up becoming a criminal defense attorney after graduating from law school at the University of Florida. (He'd been a high school baseball player at the Bolles School in Jacksonville and played a year of freshman baseball at the University of Michigan.)

Brian has such eloquence and intelligence that people listen when he talks; he's a valuable member of the Jay Fund board of directors. He's also extremely funny in a dry way, and, without crossing the line into disrespect, he can really go on a roll about people, making me laugh so hard I have to sit down. He lives in the Jacksonville area with his wife, Susan, who went to Michigan with him and is as much of a Go Blue fanatic as he is. They have three children: Caroline May, Wesley Patrick, and Ally Ann.

Kate was the baby of the family, born in 1981. Likely because of this, she developed the ability to make herself heard: Kate isn't afraid of telling anyone in our family exactly what's on her mind or asking us tough questions we might not want to think about but *should* think about, like on health matters—and I respect her a ton for this quality. She's so direct about everything because she cares so much about all of us. If anyone in the family needs anything, she's there immediately.

She has always been the best of friends with Judy, maybe because she's the youngest and came along when we were a little bit older and more relaxed as parents. From the time she was a little girl, she and Judy did everything together: When Judy went to have coffee with the neighbors, Kate was there. When Judy went shopping, Kate was there—and the two of them were so skilled at finding any item you might need that I called them "professional shoppers."

She was an athlete at Bolles, too, playing softball and basketball. When it was time for college, the only school she wanted to go to was Boston College, because she'd had such a wonderful time growing up around the university. At BC she was a psychology major—when we get together as a family, I always remind her to refrain from diagnosing people at the table, because, Lord knows, there's plenty to diagnose.

At BC, she met her husband, Chris Snee. Now they live in New Jersey and have four children:

Dylan Coughlin, Cooper Christopher, Walker Ryan, and Hartley Ann. I have no idea how she and Chris do all the driving required to get to all their kids' sports games, but I admire the incredible sacrifices they make.

These are our children. I couldn't be prouder of who they are, the spouses they've chosen, and the families they're raising. And the reason they're that way is Judy.

———

Here's what Judy loved doing more than anything in the world: When each of our twelve grandchildren were babies, she would take them in her arms, look them in the eye, call them by name, and tell them she loved them. The grandkids loved it as much as she did.

Judy can't do that anymore. By now, many readers know about Judy's disease and how it has devastated our family since her diagnosis in 2020. I wrote about it in the *New York Times*, and NBC did a feature on us before Super Bowl LVI. It's called Progressive Supranuclear Palsy. She can no longer walk or speak. The illness has ruthlessly attacked her brain, depriving her of her ability to control body movements and think. She requires round-the-clock care, and I'm her caregiver, joining a club of fifty million Americans who are unpaid caregivers for a loved one. (I'm fortunate to be able to afford professional caregivers to help; I know most people in my situation aren't so fortunate.)

For decades, while I pursued my career and worked around the clock, Judy had been looking forward to a period in our lives where I'd be retired and we could enjoy our time together. The disease has stolen that from her. As for me, the disease has stolen my wife from me while she's still alive.

Her initial symptoms were subtle, but it got to a point where she couldn't respond verbally to what people were saying. Instead, she'd just sit there with her eyes open, frustrated that she couldn't express herself. We consulted with doctors and ultimately we wound up at the Mayo Clinic, where a doctor delivered the devastating news to Keli and me. Judy's disease is incurable, and, as the name suggests, it's progressive. The doctor warned us it would get worse quickly, and it has.

Judy used to begin every day with a forty-five-minute walk on the beach, and then tend to her rosebushes and household tasks. Now, she's confined to her bed or her wheelchair. We turn on the Hallmark Channel for her, or sometimes we put on Celine

Dion or Josh Groban music, hoping to soothe her. She used to love swimming in the ocean with her grandkids—remember, she swam across Cayuga Lake as a girl—so now I position her wheelchair on the deck looking out on the ocean. Sometimes, I rent a van that's specially equipped to accommodate her wheelchair, and we take her to Mayport so she can watch the boats come in, or drive her around the mansions of Ponte Vedra Beach. On her good days, you can see on her face that she's enjoying it, to some extent at least.

The bad days are hard, though. You can tell from the first moments in the morning with her: She'll resist eating or drinking, or her face doesn't register anything. It guts me every time. I feel like a failure, like I'm not doing my job, like I'm letting down the person who has done more for me than anyone else. Anger and frustration overtake me, and my day is shot, just like that. In my head I know better, and I tell the other caregivers not to be so hard on themselves, that it's okay, that there's no manual for this, that it's nobody's fault. I'm trying to convince them but I'm also trying to convince myself.

My whole life, I had prided myself on my preparation. But nothing prepares you for watching a loved one slip away, and nothing prepared me for this job—the most important job of my life. I was completely lost, both emotionally and practically speaking. If, say, the air-conditioning broke, or the generator didn't come on during a storm, I had no idea what to do. I'd get frustrated, and in those early days, I'd find myself saying, *I shouldn't be doing this. I don't belong here.*

It's still tough. The repetitiousness of everything is mind-numbing; I lose my sense of time and self. I'm mentally and physically exhausted. But as time has passed, I've been able to draw on some of the virtues I've tried to embody my entire career and my entire life. Those are the same virtues shown by the 2007 Giants.

The first is team—and Judy and I have been a team from the moment we started dating during my junior year of high school. She stood beside me for my entire career, taking care of me in so many ways, and now it's my turn to take care of her. Despite her disease, I can tell that she recognizes me: Her eyes light up when she sees me for the first time every morning, and there are certain moments where only I can comfort her. She is my teammate. I will be there for her.

The idea of perseverance is another big one: I wake up every morning with the goal of making each day the best for Judy it can possibly be, no matter the obstacles. The tunnel vision that I brought to coaching is more necessary now than ever. So is the discipline, scheduling, and attention to detail: I'm up at six in the morning to prepare her smoothie, as well as her ice, fruit, and spoonful of honey. Everything is on a strict schedule, and no aspect of her care can be missed. With so much that's out of my control, there's no excuse for not controlling the aspects I can.

I'd always thought the Super Bowls we won in New York were the culmination of a life lived in service to these values. But no—these times with Judy are the culmination. The difference is that unlike those championship seasons, there's no happy ending in sight here. That makes it hard to find the strength every morning to keep going.

What sustains me is that by speaking out, I'm hoping to help people. There are fifty million Americans just like me. Attention must be paid to what they're going through. There's the emotional impact, of course, but also the financial one: I've spent a great deal of money on professional caregivers and other expenditures associated with this disease, and I will no doubt spend a lot more. I'm aware that very few people have these resources, and our government and health care system need to do a much better job of helping those people. I hope that by raising awareness, I'll help push things in that direction.

You never know what a person or family is going through. This is the founding belief of the Jay Fund, my charity supporting families with children who have cancer, named after Jay McGillis, my starting strong safety at Boston College whose tragic 1992 death from leukemia at age twenty-one changed my life. According to the National Children's Cancer Society, dealing with childhood cancer costs a family an average of $833,000, taking into account medical costs and lost wages. Your typical family simply can't deal with that kind of blow—and that's where we step in. As of this writing, we've supported more than five thousand families with children tackling cancer, providing more than $16 million. I'm proud of the work we've done, but it's never enough. Just like being an NFL head coach, and just like being a full-time caregiver, the work never stops. Nowadays, in addition to taking care of Judy, the Jay Fund is the focus of my life.

All of it is consistent with the values I learned while growing up in a four-bedroom house with ten family members, with enough money to get by but nothing extra. It's consistent with the values Col. Greg Gadson expressed in a Washington, DC, hotel to the 2007 Giants, when we were 0-2 and nobody in the world believed in us except for us:

Being there for your people. Team above self. Sacrifice in the name of a greater good. Mental toughness. Never, ever giving up.

Those values brought me and my team to the top of the mountain in 2007. As life has gone on, those values have gotten even more important.

ACKNOWLEDGMENTS

Tom Coughlin

I am grateful for the New York Giants fans, and for all fans who are passionate about pro football at its best. It's the fans who give so much meaning to our profession. I believe Super Bowl XLII is the greatest Super Bowl ever. This game is for them.

I'm grateful to Wellington Mara and Bob Tisch for bringing me to the Giants. Their spirits remain alive in this proud organization. I will forever feel a deep connection, and owe a debt of gratitude, to the entire Mara and Tisch families.

Winning a championship only happens if everyone in the entire organization does their job to the best of their abilities. My coaching staff with the 2007 Giants worked their tails off around the clock. I am privileged to call these dedicated coaches my colleagues: Offensive Coordinator Kevin Gilbride; Defensive Coordinator Steve Spagnuolo; Special

Teams Coordinator Tom Quinn; Assistant Special Teams Coordinator Thomas McGaughey; Quarterbacks Coach Chris Palmer; Offensive Line Coach Pat Flaherty; Assistant Offensive Line Coach Dave DeGuglielmo; Running Backs Coach Jerald Ingram; Wide Receivers Coach Mike Sullivan; Tight Ends Coach Mike Pope; Defensive Line Coach Mike Wauffle; Linebackers Coach Bill Sheridan; Secondary/ Cornerbacks Coach Peter Giunta; Secondary Coach/ Safeties David Merritt; Strength and Conditioning Coach Jerry Palmieri; the late Assistant Strength and Conditioning Coach Markus Paul; Offensive Quality Control Coach Sean Ryan; and Defensive Quality Control Coach Andre Curtis.

The players on the 2007 Giants embodied the values I cherish the most. They were physically and mentally tough. They showed great perseverance in the face of adversity. They were at their best when their best was needed. They played for each other— and now their names are etched together in sports history: Jay Alford; Chase Blackburn; Kevin Boothe; Kevin Boss; Ahmad Bradshaw; Plaxico Burress; James Butler; Barry Cofield; Jerome Collins; Torrance Daniels; Russell Davis; Zak DeOssie; David Diehl; Kevin Dockery; Reuben Droughns; Jeff Feagles; Madison Hedgecock; Domenik Hixon; Brandon Jacobs; Michael Johnson; Adam Koets; the late Jared Lorenzen; Sam Madison; Eli Manning; Michael

Matthews; Kareem McKenzie; R. W. McQuarters; Kawika Mitchell; Sinorice Moss; Shaun O'Hara; Antonio Pierce; Geoffrey Pope; Fred Robbins; Aaron Ross; Grey Ruegamer; Rich Seubert; Steve Smith; Chris Snee; Michael Strahan; Dave Tollefson; Amani Toomer; Reggie Torbor; Justin Tuck; Lawrence Tynes; David Tyree; Osi Umenyiora; D. J. Ware; Corey Webster; Guy Whimper; Gerris Wilkinson; Gibril Wilson; Anthony Wright; and Manuel Wright.

Of course, this book, and winning Super Bowl XLII, would not have happened without the people who assembled the team. Thanks to the front office during that era, including General Manager Ernie Accorsi, General Manager Jerry Reese, and Assistant General Manager Kevin Abrams. The player personnel and scouting departments were instrumental as well: Director of Pro Personnel Dave Gettleman; Director of College Scouting Marc Ross; Assistant Director of College Scouting Jerry Shay; Executive Scout Joe Collins; Executive Scout Jeremiah Davis; Executive Scout Steve Verderosa; Scout Stephen Devine; Scout Donnie Etheridge; Scout Ryan Jones; Scout Steve Malin; Scout Chris Pettit; Director of Research and Development Ray Walsh, Jr.; Blesto Scout Christopher Watts; and the late Scout Emeritus Harry Hulmes.

There is so much more that goes into a winning organization than coaches and players. Everyone in the building during the 2007 season contributed. Super Bowl XLII, and this book, is theirs as well.

My "upstairs team" did every essential task for me and others. Without these people, I wouldn't have been able to do my job: Assistant to the Head Coach Kim Koble, Coaches Assistant Chris Pridy, and Assistant Video Director Ed Triggs.

The medical services and training staff: Vice President of Medical Services Ronnie Barnes; Assistant Head Athletic Trainer Steve Kennelly; Coordinator of Rehabilitation Byron Hansen; Assistant Athletic Trainer Leigh Weiss; the late Athletic Trainer John Johnson; Team Physician Dr. Russell F. Warren; Team Physician Emeritus Dr. Allan Levy; Associate Team Physician Dr. Scott A. Rodeo; Associate Team Physical Dr. Bryan Kelly; Associate Team Physician Dr. Kameno Bell; Team Dentist Dr. Hugh Gardy; and Team Nutritionist Heidi Skolnik.

The public relations staff, including Vice President, Communications Pat Hanlon; Director of Public/Media Relations Peter John-Baptiste; Assistant Director of Communications Avis Roper; and Assistant to the VP of Communications and the VP of Medical Services Phyllis Hayes.

The community relations people on our team do a fantastic job. Director of Community Relations Allison Stangeby has always been tremendous in her support for the Jay Fund, especially the Sundae Blitz events at the stadium, during which we're privileged to give kids and their families a day off from cancer. Allison's intelligence, cooperative spirit, sense of humor, and sincere love of what she's doing make her a great person to work with.

Many thanks also to Assistant Director of Community Relations Ethan Medley and Community Relations Coordinator Jennifer Conley.

There are so many others in the organization who were a part of that season: Giants.com Senior Writer/Editor Michael Eisen; Vice President and Executive Producer Don Sperling; Manager of Special Events Jeff Conroy; Broadcast Production Manager Stephen Venditti; Production Coordinator Christine Baluyot; Senior Director of Football Information Jon Berger; Video Director Davit Maltese; and Assistant Video Director Carmen Pizzano. Our great equipment people, including Equipment and Locker Room Manager Ed Wagner Jr.; Equipment Director Joseph Skiba; and Assistant Equipment Manager Ed Skiba. Our security people, Mike Murphy and Vinnie Byron. And Director of Player Development Charles Way and Player Development Coordinator Ashley Lynn.

Karen Hart, my communications consultant, was instrumental in making this book happen. Karen is extremely well connected, and everyone respects her. Perhaps most important, she's objective and unafraid to tell the truth. I've relied on these qualities of hers for years.

Throughout my career, I've stressed that success in football comes down to believing in the idea of *team*. Well, the same is true in life. My family is the best team I could possibly imagine. I'll never be able to repay the support and encouragement they've given me all those years, during which we moved homes about a dozen times. Their love and trust have meant everything to me.

My daughter and son-in-law Keli and Chris Joyce, and their children, Marin and Clara.

My son and daughter-in-law Tim and Andrea Coughlin, and their children, Emma, Shea, and Brennon.

My son and daughter-in-law Brian and Susan Coughlin, and their children Caroline, Wesley, and Aly.

My daughter and son-in-law Kate and Chris Snee, and their children Dylan, Cooper, Walker, and Hartley.

And my wife, Judy.

Without her, none of this is possible. Anyone who's ever met Judy knows that in our family, she's the true champion.

Greg Hanlon

This book wouldn't exist without Karen Hart, Coach Coughlin's communications consultant and my friend. In her understated, friendly way, Karen has a tremendous ability to make things happen. This book is one of many examples.

Sean Desmond, our editor at Grand Central Publishing, took a chance on a Giants project despite being a Cowboys fan. Sean's edits were wise, and he displayed the patience of a saint as we lurched forward putting the finishing touches on the book. We're all indebted to Sean and his terrific editorial assistant, Zohal Karimy, and the whole team at Grand Central.

Years ago, Glenn Stout helped launch my career, and his mantra stays with me to this day: *Ass in chair*. In other words, hard work is the only thing that matters, and there are no shortcuts—a sentiment Coach Coughlin would agree with.

Thank you to my unbelievable colleagues at *People* magazine, who teach me every day what it means to be a pro and to get it right. In particular, the crime squad for the year I spent on this project: Alicia Dennis, Marc Peyser, Kyler Alvord, Chris Harris, Harriet Sokmensuer, Tristan Balagtas, KC Baker, Steve Helling, Elaine Aradillas, Christine Pelisek, and Jeff Truesdell.

Thank you to my parents—Marty, Judy, and

Acknowledgments

Wayne—who saw the spark of a fan at an early age and always encouraged my passion. Whenever we walked into the bookstore, I went straight for the sports section. I wrote my school book reports on the likes of Darryl Strawberry. All of that was A-OK, just as long as I was reading, thinking, and feeling.

Thank you to my brothers, Harv and Nick, who watched *Giants Among Men* with me several thousand times. Those games of "Rollout" showed that even as kids, we intuited the lesson of Super Bowl XLII: You have to rush the passer.

Thank you to my in-laws—Eileen, Peter, Jason, Madison, and Jacob—for looking kindly on my peculiar passions and for being so supportive and loving.

Thank you to my children, Eli and Maya, who teach me every day that nothing is more important than the games we play and the fun we have. The gods will offer you chances. Know them. Take them.

Thank you to my wife, Lauren, for being so wise, empathic, and caring, and for supporting my work on this project at every turn during an extremely eventful year. Thank you for showing me that the best teams are bound together by love.

ABOUT THE AUTHORS

Tom Coughlin is a former National Football League head coach who was part of three New York Giants Super Bowl–winning teams, twice as head coach. He won his first Super Bowl while an assistant to legendary coach Bill Parcells in 1990. In 2004, he joined the New York Giants for twelve seasons as head coach, leading the Giants to victory in Super Bowl XLII and Super Bowl XLVI, both times beating the New England Patriots. Coughlin ranks as the fourteenth winningest coach in NFL history with an overall record of 170 wins.

Greg Hanlon is an editor at *People* magazine who has written for *Sports Illustrated*, the *New York Times*, and *Slate*. His writing has been anthologized in *The Best American Sports Writing*. He was a 2015 finalist in national reporting for the Livingston Awards for Young Journalists. He is the coauthor of *Watch My Smoke: The Eric Dickerson Story*.